How much
MONEY
Do I Need
TO RETIRE?

How Much Money Do I Need to Retire?

Todd Tresidder

Copyright © 2020 | Todd R. Tresidder

Published by FinancialMentor.com

ISBN: 978-1-939273-06-2 (paperback)
      978-1-939273-07-9 (ebook)

For bulk orders, please contact todd@financialmentor.com for a generous discount schedule.

How much
MONEY
Do I Need
TO RETIRE?

TODD TRESIDDER

FinancialMentor©
Financial Freedom for Smart People.

LIMIT OF LIABILITY
DISCLAIMER OF WARRANTY

ADDITIONAL BOOKS BY TODD TRESIDDER

The Leverage Equation
The Missing Tool That Unblocks your Success,
So You Can Make More By Working Less

The 4% Rule and Safe Withdrawal Rates In Retirement

Variable Annuity Pros & Cons
Surprising Truths Your Advisor Won't Tell You

Investment Fraud
How Financial "Experts" Rip You Off
and What To Do About It

Don't Hire a Financial Coach!
(Until You Read This Book)

ADDITIONAL COURSES BY TODD TRESIDDER

Expectancy Wealth Planning
Advanced Wealth Growth Strategies
to Accelerate Your Freedom

Retirement Calculator Secrets
The Coolest Calculator Tricks Nobody Ever Taught You
for Getting Your Number Right
and Securing Your Financial Future

CONTENTS

"Make everything as simple as possible, but not simpler."

- Albert Einstein

INTRODUCTION

"THE ULTIMATE SECURITY IS
YOUR UNDERSTANDING OF REALITY."

- H. STANLEY JUDD

Traditional retirement planning has failed.

- According to the *New York Times*, 75 percent
  of Americans have less than $30,000 in their
  retirement accounts, and 49 percent of middle-
  class workers will retire poor or near-poor.

- According to Hewitt Associates, four out of five
  workers will fail to meet all their financial needs
  in retirement.

- Employee Benefit Research Institute reports
  that 79 percent of workers aged 45 or older have
  less than $250,000 in savings. An astounding
  45 percent have accumulated less than $25,000
  as they approach retirement.

- And the annual Retirement Confidence Survey
  shows only 17 percent of American workers
  are confident they will have enough money to
  retire.

The evidence is overwhelming that something is wrong with traditional retirement planning. It's an old-world model in need of a major facelift.

The system is not realistic because the average individual doesn't have the skills and knowledge required to successfully execute a traditional retirement plan. Today's broken model requires you to:

- *Voluntarily save* a significant portion of your income with discipline throughout your career (8 to 30 percent, depending on the age you begin saving).

- *Develop investment expertise* to implement smart asset allocation and investment decisions.

- *Predict the future* by knowing in advance when you and your spouse will die so that you also know how long your savings must last.

- *Accurately plan* when you will end work— either voluntarily, due to sickness, or possibly because of layoffs out of your control.

- *Precisely calculate* the inflation rate for your remaining lifetime (even though trained economists can't accurately predict this number even one year into the future).

- *Correctly estimate* what your investment portfolio will return in the 10 years before you retire, the 10 years after you retire, and each subsequent decade.

- ***Never raid your retirement nest egg,*** even when adversity strikes, you get laid off, run into health problems, fund college, or get divorced.

- And then, to top it all off, you're supposed to ***manage your retirement savings*** so that you spend your last dollar as you exhale your last breath.

Nobody can successfully do all of the above. Too many factors are completely out of your control—even if you did have the skills and expertise. No wonder most workers are failing to secure their retirement!

To execute a perfect retirement plan using this traditional system, you would need the savings discipline of a celibate monk living in a brothel, investment skills that exceed most pension and mutual fund professionals, a perfectly calibrated crystal ball, and the actuarial skills of an insurance expert. *Those sound like pretty demanding standards for someone who aspires to quit work.*

And yet, every day in financial planning offices throughout the world, people are following this well-trodden path by paying a professional to get a precise calculation of the savings required to secure their financial future—their *retirement number*—and then heading out the door to try and save their way to that mythical goal.

Some planners use simple calculators to estimate this retirement number, and others use proprietary algorithms containing sophisticated simulations to produce confidence intervals. **As it turns out, the exact calculation method doesn't matter because the problem is the path itself. It's flawed, and the results prove it.**

What you may not realize is how market valuations[1] and interest rates at the start of your retirement have a greater impact on your spending power in retirement than any other factor. In fact, the most common models used in financial planning can be so wrong that you could end up underspending (or overspending) by 60 percent or more. Understanding the assumptions used in your planning model can change the entire trajectory of your retirement.

There is a better solution, and that is what this book provides.

Rather than rely on a single, fictional retirement number, what you're about to discover is three completely different approaches to answering, "How much do I need to retire?" Each method has advantages, and each has limitations, but when combined, they complement each other so that the strength of one model balances weakness in the other. The result is the complete picture you need to secure your financial future.

There's value in the traditional model if you know how to use it correctly, but that value is limited because it shows you only one aspect of a complete retirement planning picture. However, when you combine the results from that model with the results from the other two models, the entire picture is revealed that not only secures your retirement with confidence but could allow you to retire years earlier than you thought possible.

The reason three models are required is because retirement planning is, by definition, a bet on a future that can't possibly be known today. Uncertainty is an inherent part of the equation. You must get clear on this fact, and learn how to work around it because you only get one chance at retiring securely. There's no room for error or self-deception. **The price of being wrong is intolerably high.**

The good news is I've been teaching this three-model approach to financial coaching clients and reaping the benefits in my own retirement since 1997, so I can tell you it has stood the test of time.

- Dan used this three-model approach to achieve financial independence within just three short years when traditional methods had him laboring for an additional decade.

- Gary used this three-model system to create a bulletproof retirement in 16 years when he previously had no plan and little savings.

- And I used this three-model approach to secure my financial independence more than 20 years ago—at the ripe old age of 35.

The point is that what you'll learn in this book works, and it's completely different from the conventional wisdom. This is a robust, actionable, clear approach to retirement planning that has withstood extreme financial markets and a variety of economic conditions. It may not be as neat and tidy as the *magic number* formula spewed out of a retirement calculator, but it has proven itself effective for hundreds of my coaching clients, thousands of readers, and it can work for you too.

Warning! Potholes Ahead

Before you get started, I must warn you about three common mistakes so you don't fall into the same traps as many other readers.

It Doesn't Have to Be Complex to Work: These models appear so simple that you might be tempted to assume they're incomplete. Yes, there's behind-the-scenes mathematical complexity that drives seemingly simple solutions, but there's no practical value in confusing the two. Experience from decades of coaching clients has shown the key to success is to focus on the few critical factors that actually determine the outcome. As Albert Einstein stated, "Make everything as simple as possible, but not simpler."

More Information Doesn't Mean More Accuracy: The second mistake nearly everyone makes when calculating their retirement number is to pursue additional data in a futile attempt to increase accuracy. It's logical to think that greater input will lead to more accurate output. However, inviolable math proves otherwise. Retirement planning obeys Pareto's Law, which states that 80 percent of the effects come from 20 percent of the causes. Getting distracted by that unimportant 80 percent may cause you to overlook the few key numbers that actually determine your success or failure. This book focuses your attention on the important 20 percent that makes or breaks the overwhelming majority of your results. Paying attention to the critical *causes* is what will secure your financial future.

Expecting More from This Book than *Your Number*: The final mistake is misunderstanding the focus of this book. I've purposely excluded topics like long-term care insurance, strategies on when to begin social security benefits for maximum payout, Roth conversions, IRA rollovers, asset allocation, and Medicare supplemental insurance because this book is exclusively about *how much money you need to retire*. It's not the complete guide to retirement planning.

Yes, these topics are important to retirement planning, but they would detract from this book's focus. Knowing how much you need is the essential foundation on which every other aspect of retirement planning is built. Everything else can be added later.

Finally, you may find it helpful to grab your free downloadable guidebook included with this book purchase. It's filled with printable worksheets to help you complete the exercises and model your retirement plan. Please go to https://financialmentor.com/free-stuff/retirement-book so you can claim your copy now. It makes everything fill-in-the-blank simple.

Okay, it's time to begin calculating how much money you need to retire.

Let's start with the conventional model.

MODEL 1

CONVENTIONAL RETIREMENT PLANNING, THE SMART WAY

PART 1

WHAT IT COSTS TO LIVE A GREAT LIFE IN RETIREMENT

"We succeed only as we identify in life, or in war, or in anything else, a single overriding objective, and make all other considerations bend to that one objective."

- Dwight D. Eisenhower,
former US President and army general

Do you want to be able to maintain your standard of living in your golden years?

If you plan your retirement finances the smart way, you can enjoy a future filled with travel, family, adventure, and hobbies. You can focus your life on whatever makes you happy, without concern for how to pay for it. However, if your plan comes up short, the alternative could be worrying about how to stretch your limited income, unfulfilled dreams, and waiting on your social security check just to buy groceries.

Of course, you want the first choice, but how do you get there?

The starting point is to calculate your *number*, that

theoretical pile of investment capital you're supposed to accumulate to secure your financial future.

Written Goals Create Action That Produces Results

Estimating your retirement number sets a goal, and the act of planning and setting goals has benefits. The goal doesn't even have to be accurate. It just has to point in the right direction because having a goal is a necessary condition for reaching it. For example, you're far better off striving toward a savings goal of one million dollars (even if the accurate savings goal is two million dollars) than never setting the goal in the first place.

That's because setting your goal usually acts as a wake-up call resulting in your taking more action than you would without a specific objective. It gives you something concrete to work toward. Don't worry about perfecting your goals in the early stages of retirement planning because perfection is the enemy of good enough. You can always correct and adjust later as you learn more. The key is to start now by calculating your retirement number, any reasonably plausible retirement number will do.

For example, you probably know that you need to save for retirement, but how much, and by when? Or maybe you believe social security and your company pension will suffice, but you aren't really sure. A lack of clarity will produce unreliable results. Until you actually do the math and calculate your number, you really have no clue.

However, everything changes and your retirement goals are made concrete once you calculate your number and reverse engineer your monthly savings requirements based on your age, existing savings, and expected retirement date. For example, if your calculation shows a $250,000 shortfall with retirement in five years, it's simple to divide five into $250,000 and realize you need to increase savings by roughly $50,000 per year. No more guesswork. You simply take the difference between your "How much is enough?" number by subtracting it from your current savings, and it tells you in no uncertain terms what is required.

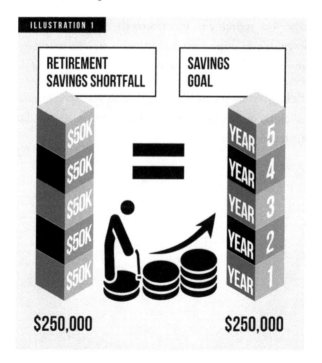

ILLUSTRATION 1

RETIREMENT SAVINGS SHORTFALL

SAVINGS GOAL

$50K
$50K
$50K
$50K
$50K

=

YEAR 5
YEAR 4
YEAR 3
YEAR 2
YEAR 1

$250,000

$250,000

According to the Retirement Confidence Survey published by the Employee Benefit Research Institute (https://bit.ly/2Kr4e2w), only 42 percent of workers have ever tried to determine their retirement savings needs. That's a shame because nearly half of those who did calculate their number took actions to increase their savings by contributing more to retirement plans or changing investment strategies.

In other words, setting a goal is an effective exercise that can get you into action. It eliminates the uncertainty around what you should be doing each month and converts it into clearly defined actions you can take to secure your retirement. It converts the unknown into the known. It's an important and valuable step in retirement planning. In fact, it's essential.

Let's begin the process of setting retirement savings goals by looking at the questions you must answer to calculate your retirement number.

PART 2

IT'S ALL ABOUT THE ASSUMPTIONS, NOT THE CALCULATOR

THERE ARE MANY METHODS FOR PREDICTING THE FUTURE. FOR EXAMPLE, YOU CAN READ HOROSCOPES, TEA LEAVES, TAROT CARDS, OR CRYSTAL BALLS. COLLECTIVELY, THESE METHODS ARE KNOWN AS "NUTTY METHODS." OR YOU CAN PUT WELL-RESEARCHED FACTS INTO SOPHISTICATED COMPUTER MODELS, MORE COMMONLY REFERRED TO AS "A COMPLETE WASTE OF TIME."

- SCOTT ADAMS, CREATOR OF "DILBERT"

Retirement planning is simple on the surface:

- You start by figuring how much income you need in retirement based on your estimated spending.

- Then you subtract how much income you'll get from pensions, social security, and other investments to determine your income shortfall.

- To cover that shortfall, figure how much you can safely withdraw from savings accounts without the risk of outliving your money.

- The withdrawal rate and income requirement mathematically determine how much money you need to save to retire, so you don't run out of money before you run out of life.

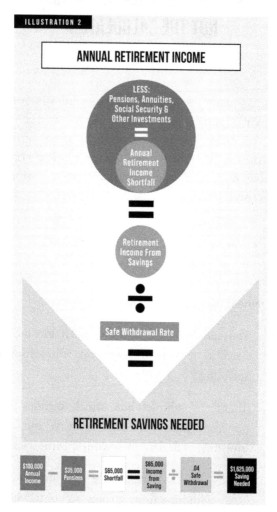

ILLUSTRATION 2

ANNUAL RETIREMENT INCOME

LESS:
Pensions, Annuities,
Social Security &
Other Investments

=

Annual
Retirement
Income
Shortfall

=

Retirement
Income From
Savings

÷

Safe Withdrawal Rate

=

RETIREMENT SAVINGS NEEDED

| $100,000 Annual Income | − | $35,000 Pensions | = | $65,000 Shortfall | = | $65,000 Income from Saving | ÷ | .04 Safe Withdrawal | = | $1,625,000 Saving Needed |

It's a relatively straightforward algorithm that almost any retirement calculator can complete. All it does is project your investment growth and expenses into the future. However, there's much more to this calculation. In fact, there are seven critical questions you must correctly answer so that your retirement savings estimate is accurate.

They are:

1. What amount of money will you spend every year from the day you retire until the day you die?

2. What will be the inflation rate during your retirement years?

3. When will you and your spouse die?

4. How much money will your company pensions and social security pay throughout your retirement?

5. What will be the growth rate of your investments over your remaining lifetime?

6. What will be the sequence of those investment returns—good years in the beginning followed by bad years, or vice versa?

7. What age will you and your spouse retire—regardless of whether it is voluntary, due to unexpected sickness, or due to forced layoffs out of your control?

Not to be a pessimist, but can you see why this is not the exact science that books, calculators, and financial planners have led you to believe? Hidden behind the scientific facade of computers and mathematics are some big assumptions. None of these questions can be answered with certainty, yet all of them require accurate answers or your estimate for how much money you need to retire will be wrong.

Unless you have a crystal ball, you can't possibly know how long you'll live, what inflation will be, what the government is going to do with social security, or what will happen to your investments in the future. Nobody even knows what will happen next year, not to mention 30 years from now. Change just one of these inputs significantly and the amount you need to save for retirement will change dramatically—sometimes by as much as two to three times your original estimate.

Your Retirement Number Is Only as Accurate as the Assumptions Behind It

Retirement calculators require accurate answers to these seven questions to provide you with precise savings and spending goals for retirement. Yet, none of these questions can be answered accurately. *Clearly, there is a fundamental problem with the entire process.*

The reality is retirement planning isn't the science you'd like it to be. Financial advisors provide their clients with simple-to-understand retirement projections filled with pages of detailed pro forma forecasts. Unfortunately, these plans are precise but not necessarily true. They can't be. It's impossible.

Let me be clear: I don't oppose the use of calculators— only the *misuse* of them. The rare but essential skill required is knowing how to use them wisely and how to interpret their output correctly. That's what I will teach you in this book.

There is value in working with retirement calculators. They allow you to do long-term planning far beyond what could be done without these tools. Their use is a decent starting point because they convert a mathematically complex task that most people would never tackle into something simple enough to accomplish. However, you must be clear on the limitations of this kind of planning process if you want to properly secure your financial future.

For example, consider a hypothetical retirement plan for a 45-year-old with $1,000,000 in assets who wants to retire with $10,000 per month at age 65. If you vary his inflation and investment return assumption by just a single percentage point, it will cause the required savings estimate to change from a $558,000 shortfall to a $1,747,000 surplus!

That's a big deal because there's no possible way to estimate your inflation and investment accurately within one percentage point for 45 years into the future: Yet, the results using this model show it will make or break your retirement security if you get it wrong.

It's Not About the Calculator: It's About the Assumptions

Some people claim the solution is to use more sophisticated calculators. For example, Monte Carlo[2] calculators randomize investment returns producing confidence intervals[3] and other highly respected calculators "backcast"[4] through actual market history. However, the differences in using specific calculators are small compared to the similarities. All calculators produce statistically similar results because they make the same assumptions.

Some calculators require more information depending on their sophistication, while others work with less information because they assume answers to some of the inputs. In the end, they're more similar than different because they're all calculating the same thing in roughly the same way using roughly the same input. *The key is not which calculator you choose but which assumptions you choose to use with the calculator.* That's what will make or break the accuracy of your estimates.

If assumptions are the key, then how do the financial planners and academics who live and breathe these questions choose assumptions? Amazingly, they select expediency over accuracy by applying historical averages. This solution sounds logical on the surface, but it's dangerously misleading.

Will You Retire in an "Up-Decade" or a "Down-Decade?"

For example, many calculators assume an 8 percent annual return for your investment portfolio with 3 percent annual inflation. The problem is that assumptions like these are based on historical long-term averages that have little relationship to the results you'll experience during your actual retirement—*which is the only thing that matters.*

Assuming stocks will return 8 percent every year because that's what they averaged for the last 100 years is seriously misleading when actual returns can (and will) vary widely from that average estimate. The average is the exception. The next 10 years of investment returns will have little or no relationship to average returns[5] for the past 100 years. There have been many 10-year periods where the markets lost money after factoring in inflation as well as 10-year periods where investment returns were much higher than average. The decade you experience at the start of your retirement will make or break your financial security (it's called *sequence of returns risk*, and is explained later in this book).

The same is true with inflation. Some calculators assume 3 percent when, in fact, it has varied widely. In other words, it's not as simple as the experts make it look with their "average assumptions" solution.

While this may sound discouraging, please don't despair. Every act of creation is first an act of destruction. In the next several chapters, I address each of the seven questions listed at the start of this chapter individually. We will solve the assumptions problem to the best of our ability and provide shortcuts and workaround solutions to every question.

The first solution you'll apply is a range of inputs with which you're comfortable so you can calculate a reasonable confidence interval for your retirement savings requirements. This confidence interval salvages the usability of the traditional model by defining a range of possible retirement futures. It isn't a perfect solution, but it's still a necessary step because it teaches essential principles about your retirement number not found any other way.

By the time you're halfway through this book, you'll have the best solution available for designing a traditional asset-based retirement plan. Once you fully understand this first model, then you'll build on that foundational knowledge with two additional models. Each provides alternative "next step" perspectives on how much money you need to retire. The combination of the three models will give you a complete picture to secure your retirement.

PART 3

THE FIVE ESSENTIAL QUESTIONS

"THE CURSE OF MODERN TIMES IS THAT ALMOST EVERYTHING
DOES CREATE CONTROVERSY."

- HORACE WALPOLE,
ENGLISH ART HISTORIAN AND POLITICIAN

QUESTION 1: HOW MUCH INCOME DO YOU NEED TO RETIRE?

The amount of income you need during retirement appears to be a simple question at first, but it's shrouded in controversy, like all the assumptions that go into calculating your retirement number.

The traditional model in financial planning assumes you need 75 to 85 percent of your working income to support your lifestyle during retirement. The expectation is that your expenses will drop during retirement because you won't buy professional clothes, commute, or incur other work-related costs. You also won't need to save for retirement any longer.

All that may be true, but it's equally valid that your expenses may rise during retirement rather than fall. In the early years, while you are healthy, you may lead a very active lifestyle with travel, outdoor recreation, golf, and other leisure expenses. It costs money to have fun, and those increased expenditures could easily exceed what you save from dropping work-related expenses. This is particularly true for those who retire young or in good health.

Additionally, as you get older, it's reasonable to expect increasing healthcare costs. For example, the average nursing home stay can run more than $74,000 per year and could increase to over $150,000 per year by 2030, assuming annual inflation of 3 percent. Unless you have long-term care insurance to cover this major expense, just one spouse needing this type of care could easily wipe out any savings from reduced spending elsewhere. In short, it's entirely possible for you to spend significantly more than your current earned income after you retire.

WHAT THE RESEARCH SHOWS

Fortunately, this question has been thoroughly researched, providing you with a robust framework so you don't have to guess.

Ty Bernicke, who analyzed data from the US Bureau of Labor's Consumer Expenditure Survey and published his research in a 2005 article in the *Journal of Financial*

Planning, found that retirees spend less, not more, during retirement.

As people age, their spending declines in every major expense category except healthcare, the data showed. The difference between generations isn't small: The average 75-year-old spends roughly 50 percent less than the average 45 to 54-year-old. A previous study by Tacchino and Saltzman (*Journal of Financial Planning*, 1999) came to similar conclusions, showing 65 to 74-year-olds spend 26.5 percent more than those over 75. More recent research continues to cite and reinforce these early studies, demonstrating a reduction in spending for each decade of life from 55 to 75 of approximately 25 percent. On the surface, this would appear to substantially reduce the amount of savings required to retire.

However, before you go off and crack open the champagne, it's important to understand how statistics can deceive. One thing to consider is that Bernicke's numbers exclude long-term care expenses. Those expenses can be alleviated with long-term care insurance, but if you don't have it, then a nursing home can change your numbers in a heartbeat—literally.

(I offer lots of free resources related to these topics on my website. You can learn more about life insurance at https://financialmentor.com/life-insurance and annuities at https://financialmentor.com/annuities.)

Also, Bernicke's numbers assume averages, which could have little relevance to your life. You may incur unexpected expenses or contract a chronic illness early in your retirement. If something catastrophic happens, and your budget is based on lowering your expenses as you age, then you have no wiggle room. You're stuck, and that would not be a good thing.

Finally, and most importantly, Bernicke's numbers are in constant dollars. In other words, his statistics are a snapshot in time and do not account for inflation. You cannot assume that his research implies your expenses will decline as you age because inflation may offset any reduction in spending. This one fact pretty much kills any ability to rely on his insights for your own planning since you'll be spending inflation-adjusted dollars, not constant dollars. This is a critical distinction.

To put it another way, his research compares a 75-year-old's expenses today to a 45-year-old's expenses on the same day. Unfortunately, that's not how retirement works. Relative spending between age groups is not the relevant issue. It's an interesting statistical fact, but until it's adjusted for inflation over time to represent actual dollars spent, it's meaningless from an individual planning perspective.

The 45-year-old today won't be 75 for another 30 years, so she's going to be spending inflation-adjusted dollars that'll be worth far less than they are today. Even though you might spend 25 percent less every 10 years as you age, inflation should easily wipe out all those advantages since 3 percent per year will compound to an increase in spending over that same 10 years that exceeds the 25 percent nominal reduction.

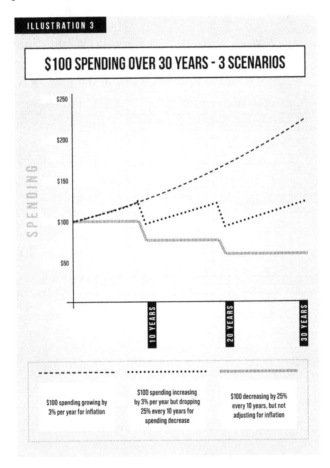

ILLUSTRATION 3

$100 SPENDING OVER 30 YEARS - 3 SCENARIOS

$100 spending growing by 3% per year for inflation

$100 spending increasing by 3% per year but dropping 25% every 10 years for spending decrease

$100 decreasing by 25% every 10 years, but not adjusting for inflation

Fortunately, David Blanchett of Morningstar resolved many of these concerns with the first longitudinal study of retirement spending patterns titled, "Estimating the True Cost of Retirement." His conclusions confirmed what these earlier studies found by showing that real (inflation-adjusted) spending does, in fact, decline with age. Specifically, his research showed:

- *Real spending* decreases slowly in the early retirement years, more rapidly in the middle years, and then slowly again in the final years. Over the ages of 60 to 90, the first 10-year period showed a roughly 1 percent per year spending decline, which accelerated to a 2 percent per year decline, and then finished with 1 percent per year decline in the final 10-year period.

- However, it's worth noting that nominal spending still increases over the entire period, assuming inflation at 3 percent per year. But the increase is less than the traditional model would indicate because inflation is mostly offset by spending declines.

- Another important conclusion was that the expected uptick in healthcare expenses during a retiree's later years was less, on average, than the sharp drop off in discretionary spending.

This tells you that it's safe to expect some level of real spending decrease throughout your retirement, particularly if you're more affluent, because you'll likely experience sharper than average discretionary spending reduction with aging. However, if you retire on a minimalist budget, then you'll have fewer discretionary expenses to cut, which could also result in less flexibility to reduce spending if you experience a shortfall at any point.

These are important conclusions because it means the traditional retirement model that assumes retirees maintain a constant inflation-adjusted level of spending in retirement results in overestimating your savings needs. As it turns out, you'll likely need less money, and that's good news!

But that good news must be tempered with an important caveat. Each individual's situation is unique, and no generic assumption will be accurate—least of all the conventional rule of thumb that assumes you'll spend 80 percent of preretirement income.

THE MOST ACCURATE WAY TO CREATE YOUR PERSONAL SPENDING PLAN

The best solution is to formulate your own budget based on your life plans and make your best guesstimate. To accomplish this, follow these five steps:

1. Start calculating your retirement spending estimate by using one full year of your current spending as the benchmark. Include all items paid annually (insurance, etc.), all holiday expenses, and everything you can think of so that it's comprehensive. Make sure you get as complete a picture as possible.

2. Adjust those spending expectations for any unique plans you have for retirement. Will you be enjoying a lot of travel and recreation during your early retirement? If so, then add those expenses into your starting budget, and pull them back out after your wanderlust is satisfied. What about paying off your mortgage? Will your health insurance costs change? Did you eliminate dry cleaning, suits, and commuting costs? Will your retirement savings contributions stop?

3. All of the research is consistent in showing it makes sense to vary spending based on your plans and age bracket. As you get older, you can expect to spend less, so go ahead and build that into your retirement plan.

4. Next, adjust your expected spending for inflation. (How to do this will be explained in the next chapter.)

5. Finally, add an assumption for long-term care costs depending on whether or not you are purchasing insurance. If you're insured, you need to include the premiums. If you aren't insured, then maybe you should add a cushion for later years to self-insure that risk. (You can learn more about insurance products on my website at https://financialmentor.com/life-insurance.)

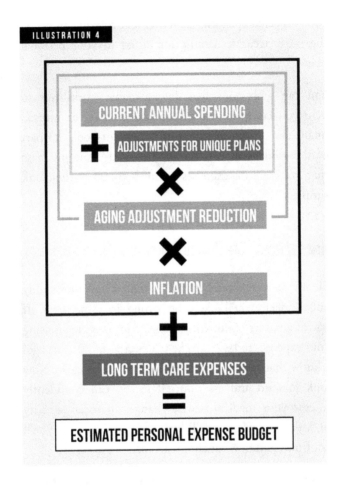

ILLUSTRATION 4

CURRENT ANNUAL SPENDING

+ ADJUSTMENTS FOR UNIQUE PLANS

×

AGING ADJUSTMENT REDUCTION

×

INFLATION

+

LONG TERM CARE EXPENSES

=

ESTIMATED PERSONAL EXPENSE BUDGET

In summary, you'll want to vary your expenses appropriately over your entire lifecycle to reflect your true expected spending during retirement—but then you must turn around and adjust those expenses. You do that by increasing the nominal dollars to adjust for expected inflation. The five-step process above walks you through your expected spending in retirement so you can create the most accurate assumption fitted to your personal plans.

You can grab your free downloadable worksheets to help you complete your spending estimate at https://financialmentor.com/free-stuff/retirement-book. It's part of the guidebook you get for free with your purchase that makes all the exercises in this book fill-in-the-blank simple.

How to Iterate Your Plan to Reduce Risk

Finally, always remember that no matter how thoroughly you budget, you'll likely be wrong in some areas. If you're not sure about this, then try to imagine guessing your expenses today from the perspective of 20 years ago. I know that my own guess wouldn't even be close. Now look forward and ask yourself if you can confidently foresee your medical needs, changes in social security or Medicare, where you'll live, what health issues you'll confront, and how much it'll all cost.

Another way to understand the unpredictability of your guesstimate for the future is to look back at where you were 10 years ago and what you were doing. Could you have anticipated your situation today? I couldn't have predicted mine.

No amount of planning or statistical analysis can overcome future unknowns. The best solution is to build your budget based on your unique plan for retirement. It won't be perfect, but there's no better alternative.

Once this budget is set, then you can correct and adjust your plan over time as the inevitable budget shortfalls and surpluses develop. In other words, **retirement planning done right is not a set-it-and-forget-it process**. As your spending changes from your estimated budget, you'll have ample opportunity to revise your assumptions regularly and then adjust as necessary to make your numbers work.

This dynamic process of updating your plan by replacing estimated assumptions with actual results minimizes the compound effect of errors. It limits those errors to brief periods, which reduces the risk of small inaccuracies compounding into catastrophic mistakes.

Simply correct and adjust your plan regularly as real-time data replaces assumptions about the future. This will ensure that your plan never strays too far off the mark. It's a simple yet powerful solution that works.

Now, let's examine in greater detail how inflation affects expense planning so you can refine your budget projections.

QUESTION 2

WHY IS INFLATION
THE SINGLE BIGGEST THREAT?

"I BELIEVE THAT BANKING INSTITUTIONS ARE MORE DANGEROUS TO OUR LIBERTIES THAN STANDING ARMIES. IF THE AMERICAN PEOPLE EVER ALLOW PRIVATE BANKS TO CONTROL THE ISSUE OF THEIR CURRENCY, FIRST BY INFLATION, THEN BY DEFLATION, THE BANKS AND CORPORATIONS THAT WILL GROW UP AROUND (THE BANKS) WILL DEPRIVE THE PEOPLE OF ALL PROPERTY UNTIL THEIR CHILDREN WAKE UP HOMELESS ON THE CONTINENT THEIR FATHERS CONQUERED. THE ISSUING POWER SHOULD BE TAKEN FROM THE BANKS AND RESTORED TO THE PEOPLE, TO WHOM IT PROPERLY BELONGS."

- THOMAS JEFFERSON,
3RD US PRESIDENT AND FOUNDING FATHER

Inflation is an insidious cancer that consumes the purchasing power of your wealth over time.

When my grandmother retired, she could have bought a new Ford Mustang for about $2,700. By the time she passed, a comparable new Ford Mustang cost more than $30,000.

Inflation is a reliable problem because it's intentionally created by government policy. Since the advent of the

Federal Reserve, the government has destroyed the purchasing power of the dollar by almost 90 percent...twice!

Traditional retirement planning typically assumes a 3 percent inflation rate. At that rate, the amount of money you must spend to maintain your current standard of living roughly doubles every 24 years. In other words, if you pay $100,000 per year right now, then you should expect to pay $200,000 per year in 24 years to support the same lifestyle. Since most people can expect to live 24 years (or longer) in retirement, this obviously is an important issue.

But where did that 3 percent assumption come from, and can you rely on it for your retirement plan? Like most everything else in retirement planning, the answer isn't as straightforward as it seems.

The 3 percent assumption is based on historical evidence. Since the late 1980s, inflation has been relatively mild, averaging 3 percent or lower. Long-term history has averaged similar.

However, during the 1970s and 1980s, inflation spent more than a decade in the 5-10 percent range. A decade is a long time. It has also spiked to the 20 percent level during wars and oil shocks, and it has been negative for isolated periods during recessions. In short, the 3 percent inflation assumption is based on such a broad interpretation of history that it overlooks details that could significantly impact your retirement plan.

What matters is the inflation you can expect in the future, not the past. And nobody knows with any confidence what future inflation will be because the past is not necessarily indicative of the future. Knowing the next 15 years of inflation would require either a crystal ball or a direct connection to a higher power. I don't have either, and neither does your financial planner.

What we do know is the rate of inflation fluctuates, so it's not realistic to simply extrapolate the recent past forward, as is standard practice. This is important because a small change in the inflation assumption will make a dramatic difference in the amount of savings required to retire.

THE SINGLE BIGGEST THREAT TO YOUR RETIREMENT SECURITY — REVEALED!

For example, a 6 percent inflation rate means your income requirements roughly double every 12 years. At a 6 percent inflation rate, a 65-year-old spending $100,000 per year today will be spending $400,000 per year at age 89 and $800,000 per year if he lives to 101. That is significant, to put it mildly. In fact, inflation is probably the single biggest threat to financial security that retirees face. It's a really big deal.

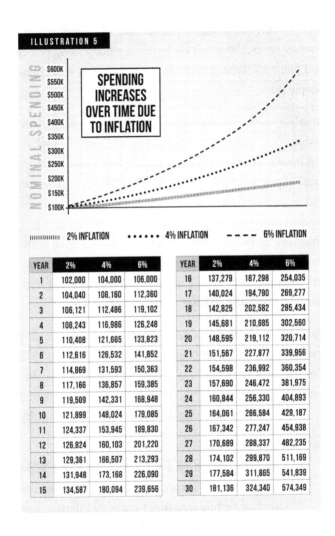

ILLUSTRATION 5

SPENDING INCREASES OVER TIME DUE TO INFLATION

NOMINAL SPENDING

ıııııııııııı 2% INFLATION   •••••• 4% INFLATION   – – – 6% INFLATION

YEAR	2%	4%	6%
1	102,000	104,000	106,000
2	104,040	108,160	112,360
3	106,121	112,486	119,102
4	108,243	116,986	126,248
5	110,408	121,665	133,823
6	112,616	126,532	141,852
7	114,869	131,593	150,363
8	117,166	136,857	159,385
9	119,509	142,331	168,948
10	121,899	148,024	179,085
11	124,337	153,945	189,830
12	126,824	160,103	201,220
13	129,361	166,507	213,293
14	131,948	173,168	226,090
15	134,587	180,094	239,656

YEAR	2%	4%	6%
16	137,279	187,298	254,035
17	140,024	194,790	269,277
18	142,825	202,582	285,434
19	145,681	210,685	302,560
20	148,595	219,112	320,714
21	151,567	227,877	339,956
22	154,598	236,992	360,354
23	157,690	246,472	381,975
24	160,844	256,330	404,893
25	164,061	266,584	429,187
26	167,342	277,247	454,938
27	170,689	288,337	482,235
28	174,102	299,870	511,169
29	177,584	311,865	541,839
30	181,136	324,340	574,349

Unfortunately, the importance of this threat is not intuitive to most people because small 1 to 2 percent changes in the annual inflation rate compound into unexpectedly large differences in purchasing power over time. Worse yet, to fully understand the impact of inflation, you have to net out its effect on both your purchasing power and your portfolio growth at the same time, which few people do.

In other words, you first have to look at how much your investments grow and then subtract the loss of purchasing power due to inflation over the same time to determine if you gained or lost net value. This is important, and eye-opening because both stock and bond markets tend to underperform during periods of rising inflation. Your investment portfolio grows less than expected at the very time that your purchasing power for those same assets declines faster than expected. The net effect of both can be devastating to your retirement plan.

To illustrate how this works in practice, let's look at a few examples using inflation statistics based on the US Consumer Price Index. We'll relate them to stock market performance using the S&P 500 Index[6] as measured by Professor Robert Shiller's data from Yale University (https://bit.ly/1qlZ47U).

- An item purchased for $100 in 1965 cost $234 in 1980 (just 15 years later). That is 5.83 percent average annual inflation for a total inflation rate over the entire period of 133.95 percent.

- Using the same period (January 1965 to January 1980), the total S&P 500 return without dividends was a mere 28.77 percent (or 1.7 percent annualized growth). With dividends reinvested, it was 125.1 percent (or 5.56 percent annualized).

- That means this popular stock index actually gained less over those 15 years than that same portfolio lost in purchasing power due to the erosive effects of inflation. (Note: The majority of investor portfolios perform worse than this index.) In other words, you were a net loser after 15 years of investment performance *that more than doubled your portfolio*, simply because of inflation.

- In fact, if you adjust the S&P's performance for inflation, the index return lost a total of 48.36 percent in purchasing power over the 15 years. The total return, including dividends reinvested, lost 9.73 percent (net of inflation). Yes, you read that right. Your investments doubled, but you lost purchasing power because of inflation. That's a serious problem if you're retired and trying to live off your assets.

- Maybe you'd argue that the time chosen was too narrow, or I was handpicking a brief period of high US inflation. Not a problem, because according to Charles Ellis in *Winning The Loser's Game: Timeless Strategies for Successful Investing,* the 1993 Dow Jones Industrial Average was equal to its inflation-adjusted level in 1928.

That means investors endured a full 65 years with no gain net of inflation.

Inflation is the single biggest threat to your retirement because it can't be accurately estimated, you have no control over its occurrence, and the *effect compounds over time, magnifying small errors into big problems.* It works like a savings account in reverse, compounding in the wrong direction, so that a mere 2 percent change in your inflation assumption could single-handedly double the amount of money you need to save for retirement. That's a life-changing difference.

Your Personal Inflation Rate Might Be Different

Before you throw in the towel, thinking that inflation will eat you alive in retirement, it's worth noting how not everyone experiences inflation the same way. Your spending patterns and where you live could mean you experience a totally different rate of inflation than national statistics.

Even the Bureau of Labor Statistics recognizes that senior citizen spending is different than the average consumer, so they created a special index called the CPI-E (for Elderly), which varies the weighting of the various components to better reflect retiree spending patterns. It reduces the weight for items like food, beverages, and transportation while increasing the weight for medical care.

In other words, the senior citizen "basket of goods" contains a lot less food than a family with hungry teenagers, but the seniors also spend more time getting medical care. This means an increase in medical costs will more dramatically impact their overall spending versus an increase in the price of milk, bread, and eggs.

The same can be said for where you live. A 2 percent increase in the cost of housing is likely to have a more significant impact on someone in New York City or San Francisco than in Kansas City or Buffalo.

Darrow Kirkpatrick, the author of *Can I Retire Yet,* has tracked nearly every dollar he's spent since 1989. His personal inflation rate doesn't mirror government data—it's not even close. He's found a few expenses are higher, many are roughly the same, and some are lower. Overall, his spending has not risen as indicated by general consumer inflation data.

This leaves you with a wide range of choices for choosing an inflation rate when calculating how much money you need to retire:

- At one extreme, you could assume future inflation will be higher than long-term history would indicate because the financial future of the country is uncertain.

- The middle road would be to assume long-term historical inflation rates figuring you have a little leeway since senior spending should be less compared to the average consumer.

- Finally, the opposite extreme would be to assume low inflation because you're in control of your spending, so you can manage your personal level of inflation through spending choices.

The best approach is to stress test your savings requirements by using a variety of expected inflation rates rather than picking a single number. The only thing you know for sure about future inflation rates is that you don't know. And the one thing you know for sure about retirement planning is you don't want to run out of money before you run out of life.

That means the prudent step when planning is to test a range of inflation assumptions so you know what inflation level your assets can support. Your high estimate will depend on how conservative you want your calculations to be and the level of security you require in retirement. Declaring any number for inflation 20 to 30 years into the future is only a guess. There are simply too many unknowns and variables. But that doesn't mean all is lost.

Reduce the Impact of Inflation Risk

Even if your estimate is wrong, the problem can be contained to a manageable level by iterating your plan, including your inflation assumption, by recalculating your number every few years. That way, you replace assumed data with actual experience.

You'll revisit your retirement calculation every few years to check your assumptions and see what you've spent. If your estimate for inflation is wrong, it's not wrong for long. You'll know for certain if your spending is rising faster or slower than your inflation estimate, and you'll know if your portfolio is performing better or worse than your investment return estimate. In other words, you reduce risk by replacing assumptions with actual data.

Each time you update your plan, you have an opportunity to adjust your lifestyle or other assumptions to balance everything and make the numbers work.

And if you don't really like this approach to making the traditional model work, then I have another planning model to help you. It's simpler, more robust, and completely tames the inflation monster without requiring any assumptions at all. But for this phase of the analysis, we're still working with the traditional model and need to include an inflation estimate. Pick a range for inflation with which you're comfortable between 2 and 8 percent (e.g., 2 to 8 percent), then write the range in your exercise workbook https://financialmentor.com/free-stuff/retirement-book) so you're ready to build your confidence interval when we start calculating your number.

QUESTION 3

WHEN WILL YOU DIE?

"IF YOU ASK WHAT IS THE SINGLE MOST IMPORTANT KEY TO LONGEVITY, I WOULD HAVE TO SAY IT IS AVOIDING WORRY, STRESS, AND TENSION. AND IF YOU DIDN'T ASK ME, I'D STILL HAVE TO SAY IT."

- GEORGE BURNS, COMEDIAN

Hmmm, let's get this straight. I'm supposed to tell the retirement calculator how long my spouse and I will live? Seriously!

Nobody knows how long they will live. In fact, you can't even venture an intelligent guess. You could die tomorrow or live to be 120.

Traditional financial planning attempts to manage this issue by consulting life expectancy tables. According to Social Security Administration data (https://bit.ly/2cf96rn), a 65-year-old man can expect to live, on average, until age 84.3 and a 65-year-old woman to age 86.7. Conservative financial planners might add 5 to 10 years to those ages to account for advances in healthcare. Others might adjust those numbers up or down based on your particular family history.

Unfortunately, this conventional approach is not a smart solution.

STATISTICS DON'T WORK WHEN YOU'RE A SAMPLE SIZE OF ONE

Using actuarial tables for life expectancy is perfectly valid for an insurance company or the Internal Revenue Service because they are dealing with large pools of people and statistical relevance, but it's not correct for you or me as individuals. You have one life and one retirement producing a binary result of dead or alive at any point in time. Nobody is 50 percent dead at age 73.

The day you die is not a probabilistic outcome. Your individual lifespan has no statistical validity. Any attempt to project a single expected lifespan (yours) based on statistical probability is fundamentally flawed, yet that's what traditional financial planning does every day.

Planning your retirement based on an actuarial table runs the risk of leaving you with more life than money, and you definitely don't want that. After all, half the population is going to live longer than expected, and you certainly hope that includes you. If you do live longer than average, you also have to make sure you have enough money to enjoy it.

Another problem with choosing standard life expectancy assumptions is the planner often fails to adapt for the differences between a single person and a married couple. Actuarial tables show there's an 18 percent chance of at least one spouse from a healthy 65-year-old couple making it to age 95. That's because a married couple has a much longer life expectancy when measured as one surviving spouse. A single person has a life expectancy that is shorter by about four to seven years, which is a material (15 to 20 percent) difference based on a conventional 30-year retirement. That means less money is required.

You Could Live a Very Long Time

Advances in healthcare and medicine result in longer life spans. What we can't predict is the impact of recent developments in biotechnology, nanotechnology, and DNA research. What has been true in the past about life expectancy is likely to go through dramatic changes in the next 30 years.

Over the twentieth century, life expectancy increased by 110 days annually, growing from 50 to 80 years. There is some debate about this statistic with some people claiming the gains came from reductions in infant mortality. Other researchers document increasing percentages of the population achieving maximum age and even claiming the first person to live to age 150 is alive right now.

According to United Nations estimates, by 2050 the over-85 population will increase sixfold, and there will be 16 times as many people over the age of 100. In 1840, there were 90 centenarians in the United States, according to US Census Bureau records—one for every 189,000 people. As of 2013, there were more than 53,000 centenarians, or one for every 5,800 people.

All of this means that longevity is increasingly important when planning a retirement nest egg that might have to last another 40 or 60 years. Assuming too short of a lifespan can result in excessively high withdrawal rates that deplete your savings before death. Conversely, an excessively conservative withdrawal rate could lead to a lower quality of life. Neither alternative is desirable, so it's critical to get this right.

Why You Can't Spend Principal

A related issue is that you can safely spend principal from savings over the entire duration of a 20-year retirement, but you can't do the same for a 40 or 60-year retirement (at least, until the last 20 years.) Make sure you read that twice because it's an essential point to understand. It's very dangerous to spend the principal from savings when retirement could be prolonged. The math simply doesn't allow it.

Let's use the analogy of a home mortgage to highlight this issue. If you compare the monthly payment on a 15-year mortgage against a 30-year mortgage, you'll notice the 15-year mortgage has a higher amortization rate (more of each payment pays principal). That's why it fully pays itself off in half the time. The same is true for a 15-year retirement versus a 30-year retirement—only in reverse. The longer the period, the smaller the amount of amortization allowed, because your savings might last only half as long if you take too much principal.

However, the critical difference between the home mortgage analogy and real-world retirement planning is that all the variables are fixed in a home mortgage, but most of the key variables in retirement planning are dynamic. Without going too deep down the mathematical rabbit hole, what that means is you can calculate a 30 or 40-year home mortgage with scientific precision down to the penny. But you can't do the same thing for retirement planning.

Even though the principles of amortization are identical, traditional retirement plans become unstable for time horizons beyond roughly 20 years because of the compound effect of many dynamic variables changing over so many years.

In theory, a 40 or 50-year retirement would allow you to spend small amounts of your nest egg each year. In reality, that simply isn't safe, given all the unknowns. There's no reliable way to do it.

This is critically important when figuring out which assumption to use for longevity. In my experience, the only logical choice is to assume a very long lifespan unless your medical and family history indicates otherwise. That means you can't safely spend the principal from savings until your final 20 years. The risk of being wrong on this issue is too catastrophic to assume any alternative.

Think about it: Failure is when you run out of money while still alive. You must guard against that outcome, making a long life the only reasonable bet worth making. Here are three acceptable solutions for managing the longevity factor in your retirement plan:

1. If you're intent on using a mortality table for estimating lifespan, don't pick the average age for death. Plan to be the outlier with a 5 percent chance of survival—which changes each year based on your current age, sex, and data source but is generally over age 95.

2. Another viable alternative is to assume average lifespan, but design your plan with your living in a fully-paid-for home for as long as you can. That way, if you run out of money or live longer than expected, you have a reserve asset (your home equity) that can be harvested to make up the shortfall, either through a reverse mortgage or selling your house.

3. A third acceptable planning alternative for managing longevity risk is to assume an average lifespan, but purchase an annuity that insures unexpectedly long lives. It only pays after you become elderly (age 85, for example) and is relatively cheap to buy because of the low probability for payout.

If you're wrong about assuming a long lifetime, then your children and grandchildren will have a delightful inheritance. If you're right, then you'll need every last penny to avoid being indigent and dependent on family or charity when you're elderly.

While frightening and exciting to think about, living past 100 doesn't have to be as big of a deal to your retirement planning as it may appear. Estimating life expectancy is only relevant when your plan requires liquidating principal (amortization) as required in the traditional retirement planning model. When we discuss other models later in this book, you'll see alternative solutions to this problem that eliminate any need for a life expectancy assumption and give you a solid measure of safety.

My suggestion is you write down your preferred strategy for managing longevity risk in your exercise workbook now while the choices above are fresh in your mind. This will ensure that you have all the answers ready-at-hand when it comes time to calculate your retirement number. You can download your free copy of the workbook at https://financialmentor.com/free-stuff/retirement-book.

QUESTION 4

HOW MUCH WILL YOUR PENSION CONTRIBUTE?

"THEY WANT THE FEDERAL GOVERNMENT CONTROLLING
SOCIAL SECURITY LIKE IT'S SOME KIND OF FEDERAL PROGRAM."

- GEORGE W. BUSH, FORMER US PRESIDENT

To determine how much income your personal savings must provide during retirement, the first thing you need to figure out is the amount of income you can expect from other sources. These other sources include company pensions, government pensions, and social security.

Of course, you may not live within the United States so you'll need to substitute the type of pensions available in your country in place of all references to social security. For example, Canadian readers would use the Canadian Pension Plan (CPP) and Old Age Security (OAS). Just check for what, if any, government pensions are available to you and factor those into the calculation in place of social security.

To determine how much savings you need, start by taking your planned expenses then subtract the income you can expect from social security and pensions. The amount left over is the total that must be covered by your savings.

ILLUSTRATION 7

How to Manage Social Security

To learn what you can expect from social security, contact them at 800-772-1213 or consult your annual wage and earnings statement. Another alternative is to use the SSA's free online retirement calculators (https://www.ssa.gov/planners/calculators/) for a personalized projection based on your actual earnings history. The average benefit, according to the Social Security Administration, is around 40 percent of your preretirement income, but your personal benefit will likely vary.

Additionally, if social security plays a prominent role in your retirement plan, then you should learn how to maximize your benefits. There are various strategies based on life expectancy and earnings history that are outside the scope of this book because it's specialized information that merits an in-depth analysis. A simple search at your favorite bookseller for the term "social security" will provide you with several excellent choices.

With that said, what role should social security play in your retirement plan? To answer that question, it's first important to understand that social security is an unfunded program. There are no assets behind it. It's merely a transfer tax from those who work to those who don't. With increasing longevity and an aging baby boomer population, social security is fundamentally unsound because fewer and fewer workers are being taxed to support more and more retirees. Demographic projections show we're rapidly heading toward a day when there'll be just two workers to support each retiree. That is problematic.

While it's politically unlikely that social security will vanish entirely, it's realistic to expect diminished benefits in inflation-adjusted terms over time. *There really is no other solution.* You will receive less than your elders, and your children will receive less than you. Recent history has shown the politically expedient way for the government to manage this problem is to raise qualification requirements and slowly inflate away the purchasing power of the nominal obligations that remain. Unfortunately, that's already occurring, and it's probably realistic to assume more of the same going forward.

What that means is if you're retiring in the next 10 to 15

years, you may consider including some of your expected social security benefits for part of your retirement. If you're behind the baby boomer generation, then it would be prudent to not count on seeing much from the system. This author is in the latter category and considers any social security payments a nice bonus, but that's all. Your situation may be different.

How Should I Manage My Company Pension?

Company pensions are another problematic issue. While government pensions (defined as state and local governments distinct from social security) still appear reliable, corporations as a general rule seem to have little conscience about defaulting on pension promises made to their retired workers. I know too many retirees who have watched helplessly as their apparent rock-solid, corporate pension benefits got cut to a fraction of their value after the company was sold, declared bankruptcy, or went through some other legal shenanigan to void the pension liability. I wish it weren't true, but that's the ugly reality for all too many pensioners.

Just to be clear, when we discuss *pensions,* we're not referring to 401(k) accounts and other forms of self-funded retirement such as IRAs, SEP-IRAs, Roth IRAs, Keoghs, or RRSPs and TFSAs in Canada. These are all part of your personal savings and are not the same thing as a pension.

A pension is the responsibility and property of a company plan administrator, and *all you get is a promise of payment from them.* This promise can be broken, which happens with unfortunate regularity—401(k)s, IRAs, and other forms of savings are owned by you. Even though both are types of retirement plans, they are as different as night and day.

For a more thorough examination of these differences and their implications, please see the free article on the FinancialMentor.com website titled "Pension Trends Say You Are on Your Own for Retirement Planning" (https://financialmentor.com/pension). It provides a complete examination of the pension system problems and how they may affect you.

In the meantime, you must make a guesstimate of your expected pension and social security benefits to determine how much income your savings will need to provide to make up the difference. That includes both tax-deferred retirement savings such as 401(k) and regular taxable savings.

The most conservative solution is to count all pension and social security benefits as a big, fat zero—a bonus if you get them but not to be relied upon. That may be a shocking stance for some long-time corporate employees, but airline and financial company workers are probably nodding in agreement; just a few years earlier, they would've been arguing the point. It's a difficult situation to face, but pension obligations are generally not as secure as you might like to believe.

Only you can decide what's appropriate for your personal situation. Some corporations have a higher probability of making good on their pension obligations, just as some government pensions are secure, but others are not. Always remember that a pension is nothing more than a promise to pay, so it's only as good as the integrity of the decision-makers and the actuarial viability of the funds they control. If company fortunes change, integrity is low or the asset pool is insufficient to meet demands, then you could get less than you were promised.

Another alternative to assuming zero for your pension is to choose a sliding scale based on your confidence in payment. Just be aware that as you increase the amount of pension and social security income in your retirement plan, you also make your financial security increasingly dependent on people and assets outside of your control. It might work out, but if it doesn't, there's not a lot you can do about it.

In summary, do your best to make a judgment call about your pension fund viability based on your age, expected retirement date, and the degree to which your company pension plan is at risk based on the strength of the company and the plan's funding. Retirement planning based on a zero payout from both social security and pensions may be excessively conservative. It could place such a sizable burden on your savings to make up the shortfall that it would push your retirement out of reach. That's why it's a judgment call that you'll have to make—and that you'll have to live with.

QUESTION 5

HOW MUCH INVESTMENT INCOME CAN YOU EXPECT?

"When a man retires, his wife gets twice the husband but only half the income."

- Juan Antonio "Chi Chi" Rodriguez,
PROFESSIONAL GOLFER

The investment return assumption is the most complex retirement planning question. In fact, it'll take four chapters to do it justice (seriously).

This first chapter highlights problems with the conventional approach. Follow-up chapters explore the latest research and provide you with an uncommon solution.

If you can't stand math and statistics and just want the solution, then you can skip to the end of the fourth chapter in this series. But I don't suggest it. The material in these next four chapters is critical to your financial security in retirement because it is diametrically opposed to conventional wisdom and well worth your consideration.

Most financial advisors would claim long-term return expectations before retirement ranging from 7 to 10 percent based on a traditional asset allocation, using a buy-and-hold investment strategy. After retirement, your traditional asset allocation is then supposed to shift away from equities toward fixed income, with return expectations dropping to a 4 to 5 percent range. That's the claim.

THE TRADE-OFFS TO ALTERNATIVE ASSET ALLOCATIONS

Alternatively, if your retirement portfolio is nontraditional, then your expected return may look completely different. This is an important point that we'll revisit later, but please take note of it. The brokerage and investment community wants you to believe a government-sponsored retirement plan (401(k), IRA, Roth IRA, etc.) stuffed with the stocks, bonds, and mutual funds they sell is the only way to go, but that's a self-serving and narrow view of reality.

The following are examples of viable investment alternatives that may merit consideration:

- You may choose to invest in rental real estate, which provides passive rental income expected to rise with inflation.

- You might be an active investor with returns based on skill and not correlated to conventional, passive investment expectations.

- Or maybe you built a portfolio of dividend-paying stocks whose income has risen every year and exceeds your expenses.

- A potential alternative for entrepreneurs is a business that is paying you annually on a long-term installment sale.

All of these are nontraditional asset allocations that many people use to successfully fund their retirement. Each has unique characteristics that can bring valuable diversification and recurring income to a conventional buy-and-hold portfolio.

Another possibility is to build your retirement portfolio with traditional assets but approach asset allocation in a nontraditional way. For example, if you retire at age 59 and have another 30 or more years of life expectancy, does it really make sense to load your portfolio with fixed income (bonds)? The danger of long-term investing in fixed income is you sacrifice the ability to preserve purchasing power by growing your portfolio faster than inflation.

Conversely, if you choose to overweight equities, then you increase the risk of losing a significant chunk of principal from your savings to market volatility. Just ask anyone who began retirement in 2000 or 2007 right before those severe market declines while holding a large stock allocation. Many of these investors now prefer to accept the near-certain risk of inflation gnawing away at their capital over the possible risk of market fluctuations wiping it out.

These asset allocation decisions are very tough questions that can make or break your prospects for retirement security yet are oversimplified by traditional financial models based on long-term average return assumptions. Only you can decide what's right for you, and a fair amount of education is required to make an informed decision.

CAN YOUR CALCULATOR MODEL YOUR RETIREMENT PLAN?

The reason I've spent so much time discussing traditional assets versus nontraditional assets is that they affect the usability of various calculators and retirement planning models for estimating how much money you need to retire. Just as financial planners have the self-serving assumption that your portfolio is comprised entirely of assets they can sell you (stocks, bonds, annuities, etc.), the models they use to calculate your retirement number assume similar portfolios.

For example, go ahead and try to plug a rental real estate portfolio into a traditional retirement calculator or Monte Carlo simulation—it doesn't work. It's like trying to fit a square peg into a round hole. However, my simplified models and retirement calculator (https://financialmentor.com/retirement-calculator) work with *any* portfolio—traditional, nontraditional, or a mix of both. This is an important advantage.

Whether you invest according to a traditional or a non-traditional model, there are no sure-fire answers to determine your expected investment return 20 to 40 years into the future. The essence of investing is putting capital at risk into an unknowable future. No assumption about average returns will resolve that. Just think back on how much has changed in your life and your investment portfolio during the last 20 to 40 years. Could you have predicted the advent of discount brokers, online trading, and commissions dropping to almost zero? Could you have predicted the 1980s gold boom and bust, the technology bubble, the real estate boom and bust, or the Dow Jones Industrial Average rising from under 1,000 to more than 10,000, only to be halved then double again?

If anything, the future is even less predictable in a world where the pace of change seems to only accelerate.

MONTE CARLO MADE SIMPLE

Monte Carlo is easy to understand, even if you're math phobic.

Put simply, Monte Carlo analysis is a way to estimate potential outcomes when one or more inputs are uncertain. Common examples include:

- How long it takes to drive across town each day under varying weather and traffic conditions.

- How many net calories you consume in a day based upon food choices, serving sizes, and exercise.

- How many people in your city will get sick from the flu this year given the unknown virulence of flu strains, vaccination rates, and seasonal weather patterns.

- And, of course, how much money you need to retire given unknown investment returns, inflation rates, and life expectancy.

The common factor in each example is how uncertain inputs make it impossible to predict a single outcome. Since you can't know what will happen precisely, a Monte Carlo analysis can estimate likely ranges for each uncertain input and then varies them in a sampling process. The result is a distribution of possible outcomes, each with statistical likelihood.

For example, let's assume you drive 17.2 miles to work each day. The distance is fixed, but many variables affect how long the commute will take. On any given day, there might be traffic jams at specific intersections, accidents blocking the road, or a bad snowstorm. Plus, there's always the small but undeniable risk that your car might break down.

A Monte Carlo analysis will sample the range of these inputs according to predefined distributions. One sample will result in a longer drive time based on the prospect of construction closing a particular street. Another sample will assume you hit red lights at every intersection. Yet another sample will model both a snowstorm and mechanical troubles with your car. Of course, the most likely scenario will model the usual traffic delays and a reliable vehicle.

The result might show, with high confidence, a commute time of 27 minutes. But it will also show the quantified risk of longer driving times when things go wrong. In addition, it will show a small chance of getting there in 23 minutes when traffic is light, and you sail through green lights at every intersection.

The fact is you can't definitively forecast a single outcome for how long it takes you to drive to work. There are too many unknowable inputs that create a range of results, all with varying likelihoods.

The upshot is that any single predicted outcome is almost certain to be wrong on any given day because of all the variable inputs. The more accurate way to predict your commuting time is to look at a range of possible outcomes and the probability of each occurring. Monte Carlo doesn't tell you what the outcome will be. However, if you estimate the range of inputs correctly, it does give you a reliable range within which the outcome should fall. Consequently, if you want to ensure you arrive to work on time at least 95% of the time, you should leave enough time to account for all but the slowest 5% of commutes the Monte Carlo analysis produces.

HISTORICAL RETURNS ARE EASY BUT NOT ACCURATE

Financial planners use historical return models (and more recently, Monte Carlo) despite all of these problems because they are expedient solutions, not because they are accurate.

What you are about to discover is that the real answers are complex. I've done my best to simplify the latest research and connect the dots for you, but it's not easy reading. It's far easier for most advisors to assume historical returns rather than try to explain how the latest research should be applied to your circumstances.

In the end, though, *your investment return expectation is a function of your investment strategy, skill, and the date you began investing.* That makes estimating your expected return more complex and nuanced.

In addition, your retirement security will be determined by the next 10 to 15 years of investment returns, so that's what matters—not the past 100 years. Long-term analysis can be hazardous for retirees because it ignores 15-year periods of flat or negative real results that are critically important to understand.

PART 4

HOW TO ACCURATELY ESTIMATE INVESTMENT RETURNS

"WE LOOK AT THE PRESENT THROUGH A REARVIEW MIRROR.
WE MARCH BACKWARDS INTO THE FUTURE."

- MARSHALL MCLUHAN, CANADIAN PHILOSOPHER

THE ONLY INVESTMENT RETURN THAT MATTERS

Picture a triangle. If any side is missing, the shape is not merely weakened—it fails to exist.

In this chapter, I'll show you a triangle that helps to explain your investment return assumption and safe withdrawal rate[7] during retirement, which is the amount you can spend each month so you don't run out of money before you run out of life. Your investment return assumption is one of the numbers that will make or break your financial security, and the three sides of the triangle that determine your expected return assumption for a conventional asset allocation portfolio are made up of valuations, volatility, and sequence of returns.

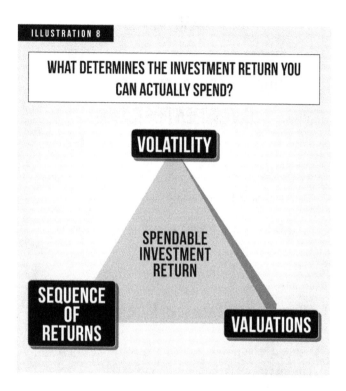

ILLUSTRATION 8

WHAT DETERMINES THE INVESTMENT RETURN YOU CAN ACTUALLY SPEND?

VOLATILITY

SPENDABLE
INVESTMENT
RETURN

SEQUENCE
OF
RETURNS

VALUATIONS

We'll examine each of these elements so you know best practices for estimating investment return, which is the center of the triangle. You'll also come to understand the underlying problems with Monte Carlo calculators and why I reject them, even though they're currently considered best practice by most financial planners.

A quick word of caution: This chapter is heavier reading than the rest of this book and includes tables of data and statistical terms. I prefer to eliminate jargon and math wherever possible to make the ideas in this book as intuitive as possible, but the concept of investment return requires specific language and numbers. It's the only way to communicate this information accurately, and accuracy is vital if we are to challenge conventional wisdom. Everything must be detailed, thoroughly explained, and proven by research to support the conclusions.

The first step in this journey is to define the three sides of this triangle. After that, we'll connect these elements into an important conclusion where the whole is greater than the sum of the parts.

VALUATIONS: HOW TO ESTIMATE 7 TO 15-YEAR EXPECTED RETURNS

Short-term investment returns of one to five-year time horizons are unpredictable. This is common knowledge and well-documented by research.

However, you might be surprised to learn that *investment returns over longer time periods of seven years or more are not random.* Knowing the time frames that allow for reasonably reliable estimates for future investment returns is critically important to your retirement planning.

More precisely, research shows that your expected investment return over 7 to 15 years for a diversified stock portfolio can be related to the market valuation at the beginning of your investment holding period[8]. And for investment holding periods over 20 years, returns reliably mean revert, or return to, the long-term average return that is often quoted, i.e., 6 to 10 percent, depending on data assumptions and time period.

That means there is actually some order to the crazy chaos of investment markets from year to year. In the short term, the market fluctuations create random chaos, but in the intermediate term, expected return relates to market valuation. In the long term, investment return approximates historical averages.

That means you can actually estimate your expected investment returns for your retirement plan by knowing (1) your estimated holding period (or time horizon) and (2) the market valuation at the beginning of that holding period. This gives you a clear framework for defining one side of the investment return triangle.

Specifically, the relevant investment holding periods that you want to pay attention to are short term (defined as less than 5 years), intermediate term (defined as 7 to 15 years), and long term (defined as 20+ years).

For our purposes here, market valuation will be simplified to mean only the S&P 500 Index price-to-earnings ratio, commonly referred to as the P/E ratio[9] or CAPE[10] ratio (Cyclically Adjusted Price Earnings ratio). Other forms of market valuation may provide more (or less) accurate results, but adding them will needlessly complicate the discussion.

Looking at the research, Plexus Asset Management examined 10-year returns on the S&P 500 from 1871 to 2007 by organizing the results into quintiles[11] based on the P/E ratio at the start of the investment holding period.

This is what they discovered:

- The most expensive 20 percent (top quintile) of 10-year periods had a beginning P/E (price divided by earnings) of 22 and an average subsequent inflation-adjusted annual return of just 3.2 percent.

- The cheapest valuation 20 percent (bottom quintile) had an average starting P/E of 8.5 and an average 10-year subsequent return of 11 percent annually.

In other words, the cheapest valuation periods had ***more than three times*** the investment return of the most expensive valuation periods. Similarly, each quintile of improving valuation showed improving returns.

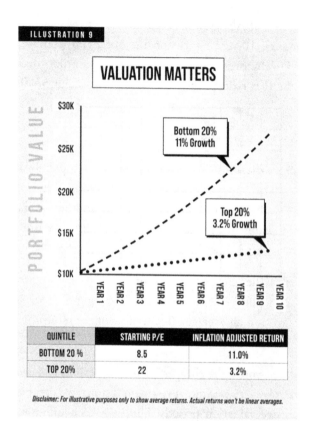

ILLUSTRATION 9

VALUATION MATTERS

PORTFOLIO VALUE

Bottom 20%
11% Growth

Top 20%
3.2% Growth

$30K
$25K
$20K
$15K
$10K

YEAR 1 · YEAR 2 · YEAR 3 · YEAR 4 · YEAR 5 · YEAR 6 · YEAR 7 · YEAR 8 · YEAR 9 · YEAR 10

QUINTILE	STARTING P/E	INFLATION ADJUSTED RETURN
BOTTOM 20 %	8.5	11.0%
TOP 20%	22	3.2%

Disclaimer: For illustrative purposes only to show average returns. Actual returns won't be linear averages.

What does that mean for your retirement plan? *The amount of return you can expect from a diversified equity portfolio is inversely correlated to the market valuation at the start of the holding period.*

If the market has higher than average valuations at the start of your retirement, then you should expect lower than average investment returns over the next 7 to 15 years. Conversely, if valuations are lower than average when your retirement begins, then you should expect higher than average investment returns over the subsequent years.

What's amazing is this phenomenon has nothing to do with market cycles or any predictive voodoo. In fact, it's really just common sense. Imagine a $100,000 house that rents for $1,000 per month. If you pay $200,000 for that same house, then it will return less for every dollar you invested. Conversely, if you pay $50,000, it will return more for every dollar you invested. The return of the house ($1,000 per month) is the same no matter how much you pay for it. But if you pay a lot of dollars for that return, the return per dollar invested is lower. Conversely, if you pay less for that return, the return per dollar invested is higher.

As it turns out, the same holds true for the stock market. The expected return is related to the price you pay relative to how much the asset earns, which is why the valuation metric we're using is the price-to-earnings or P/E ratio. It measures your earnings for every dollar you invest.

This doesn't tell you reliably what your return will be. It tells you only that high valuations beget lower than average returns, and lower valuations beget higher than average returns over subsequent 7 to 15 year time periods. That can be useful information for estimating your investment returns when calculating how much money you need to retire because you can know market valuations on the day you retire with absolute certainty.

Similar research was performed by Robert Shiller from Yale University, who isolated the 10 best and 10 worst years to be a stock investor based on subsequent 10-year returns. He found the cyclically adjusted price-earnings ratio (CAPE) for the 10 best years averaged 10.92 (well below average) with an average 10-year subsequent return of 16.1 percent compounded annually. The CAPE for the 10 worst years averaged 23.31 (way above average) with an average 10-year return of -3.3 percent. Did you notice the relationship between valuation and subsequent 10-year returns? High market valuation begets low 10-year investment returns and vice versa.

I've seen more studies on this phenomenon than I can recall from more researchers than I care to cite. It's one of the most robust statistical relationships in modern finance, and it's valid across both US and international historical data. It also holds up against a wide array of varying assumptions. In fact, you can choose almost any valuation metric, from the ever-popular P/E ratio to price/sales to Q ratio and more. I picked the studies by Plexus and Shiller because they were simple to understand and included extensive data samples. I could've just as easily cited a dozen different studies that all point to an identical conclusion.

The bottom line is valuation matters. While investment return is random in the short run, there's some order to returns when time horizons reach 7 to 15 years, which helps you estimate how much money you need to retire.

Volatility: What Part of Your Average Return Can You Spend?

Intuition would indicate that you should be able to safely spend your investment return—right? Wrong.

There are several problems with that conclusion, but for now we'll focus on one in particular: volatility drag.

Let's use the analogy of Mike Tyson, the famous heavyweight boxer, punching you in the face. The punch occurs in a brief second, but the effect—if averaged over an entire day—is the equivalent of a feather pillow brushing your face. Unfortunately, that average is very deceptive because it tells you nothing about the excruciating pain you feel when knocked unconscious. That punch is a volatile, short-term experience, and so is stock market volatility.

Financial "experts" are quick to quote average stock market returns, but those averages hide volatility and cannot actually be spent. They're a statistical aberration. The only return you can spend to support your living expenses in retirement is the compound return[12], and compound returns are reduced by *short-term* volatility.

In fact, compound returns are always less than average returns because of the way the math works as your money compounds. For example, if you lose 20 percent one year and gain 20 percent the following year, your average return is zero, but your account will actually lose money through compounding. Your $100 account drops to $80 in the first year (100 - (100 x 0.20) = 80) and then rises to only $96 in the subsequent year (80 + (80 x 0.20) = 96). This is the way volatility drag works: The bigger the investment loss (i.e., volatility), the greater the negative compounding effect on your account balance. For example, a 10 percent loss requires only an 11.1 percent gain to get back to even, but a 50 percent loss requires a full 100 percent gain to return to even.

ILLUSTRATION 10

VOLATILITY DRAG
Same Average Return = Different Compound Return

EFFECT OF DISPERSION ON 3 PORTFOLIOS ($10,000 STARTING VALUES)						
	PORTFOLIO #1		PORTFOLIO #2		PORTFOLIO #3	
STARTING		$10,000.00		$10,000.00		$10,000.00
YEAR 1	10%	$11,000.00	15%	$11,500.00	60%	$16,000.00
YEAR 2	10%	$12,100.00	25%	$14,375.00	-80%	$3,200.00
YEAR 3	10%	$13,310.00	-10%	$12,937.50	50%	$4,800.00
AVERAGE RETURN		10%		10%		10%
COMPOUND RETURN		10.0%		9.0%		-22%

EFFECT OF NEGATIVE RETURNS									
PORTFOLIO LOSSES	-10%	-20%	-30%	-40%	-50%	-60%	-70%	-80%	-90%
GAINS TO BREAK EVEN	+11%	+25%	+43%	+67%	+100%	+150%	+233%	+400%	+900%

Consider these three key ideas about volatility effects:

- Compound return is always less than average return.

- Compound return is the only return you can spend. It's what determines your portfolio value, not average returns.

- The difference between average and compound return is a function of the asset's volatility. The more volatile the investment return stream, the bigger the gap between average investment return and compound investment return.

For example, the average and compound returns for a treasury bill are nearly identical because the return stream isn't volatile. However, the stock market is a very different story. According to Ed Easterling in his book, *Unexpected Returns: Understanding Secular Stock Market Cycles*, the average return for the Dow Jones Industrial Average from 1900 to 2003 (excluding dividends) was 7.4 percent, but the compound return was only 5 percent. The difference between 7.4 percent and 5 percent may not sound like much, but over such a long time, it reduces the amount of account growth by *an astounding 90 percent* (that's not a misprint!)—from $1,000 growing to $1,676,661 to $1,000 only growing to $159,841. It's the compounded effect of these small changes over long periods that'll make or break your retirement security and defines the second side of our investment return triangle.

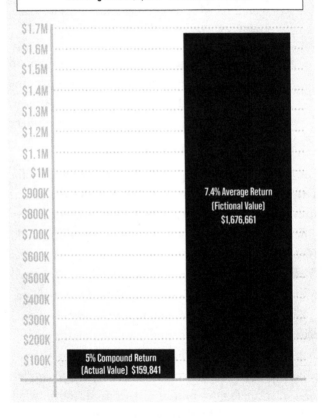

ILLUSTRATION 11

WHAT IS THE REAL STOCK MARKET RETURN?
Growth of Dow Jones Industrial Average 1900-2003
Starting Value $1,000 - Excludes Dividends

7.4% Average Return
(Fictional Value)
$1,676,661

5% Compound Return
(Actual Value) $159,841

Sequence of Returns: The Order Matters

Does the order of your investment returns affect how much you can afford to spend in retirement?

In other words, does it matter if your retirement begins with winning years versus losing years or does it all average out over the long run? Surprisingly, *the order of returns matters a lot*. It's known as *the sequence of returns risk* and is best illustrated by the following example from author William Bernstein.

Assume you have a $1,000,000 portfolio with an average return of 10 percent split evenly between 15 years at +30 percent and 15 years at -10 percent. This would give you a compound return of 8.17 percent, regardless of the returns order. Again, the compound return is less than average return due to volatility drag.

In other words, the order of returns does not affect your average return or your compound return. You could start the 30 years with 15 consecutive positive years followed by 15 successive negative years (or vice versa), or you could randomly arrange the 30 years and the effect on compound returns and average returns would be nil. You would get the same result.

ILLUSTRATION 12

3 DIFFERENT SEQUENCES OF RETURNS
Assumes No Contributions Or Withdrawals

YEAR	$1,000,000 PORTFOLIO VALUE		
	A +30% FOR 15, THEN -10% FOR 15	**B** -10% FOR 15 YEARS, THEN +30% FOR 15 YEARS	**C** ALTERNATING RETURNS OF -10% AND +30%
0	$1,000,000	$1,000,000	$1,000,000
1	$1,300,000	$900,000	$900,000
23	$22,033,849	$1,679,517	$5,061,590
24	$19,830,464	$2,183,372	$6,580,067
25	$17,847,417	$2,838,384	$5,922,061
26	$16,062,676	$3,689,899	$7,698,679
27	$14,456,408	$4,796,869	$6,928,811
28	$13,010,767	$6,235,930	$9,007,454
29	$11,709,691	$8,106,709	$8,106,709
30	$10,538,721	$10,538,721	$10,538,721

The financial lesson from this simple math is that the sequence of returns doesn't matter *as long as there are no cash flows in or out of your portfolio*. However, all of that changes when you make contributions or withdrawals from your portfolio, *which is what most investors actually do.*

This is a tremendously important fact that is generally overlooked because nearly all investment research wants to keep the analysis simple and assumes no portfolio contributions or withdrawals. This is misleading because that's not the way real-world retirements work. You add money during the accumulation phase, and you withdraw money to pay your bills after you retire. The result? *The amount of money you can afford to spend in retirement is dependent not only on your actual investment returns but also on the order of those returns.* It's a really big deal.

For example, say you are unlucky and start your retirement with 15 straight losing years. You can withdraw only 1.86 percent of your beginning portfolio balance annually to support spending, even though your average investment return is much higher at 10 percent.

Conversely, say you are lucky enough to start your retirement with 15 straight winning years. You can safely withdraw 24.86 percent annually, even though your average return is still just 10 percent.

Same annual returns, same average return, same compound return, different sequence of returns—vastly different result.

Sequencing risk causes the amount you can safely withdraw from your investments to vary from a low of 1.86 percent (in this example) to as high as 24.86 percent—more than 13 times the annual spending from the same investment portfolio. That's the difference between dining on cat food or traveling the world in comfort, and it's caused by the exact same returns occurring in a different order. Nothing else changed.

As shocking as these numbers are, it's really just common sense when you think about it. Imagine 15 years of no net investment gain while still withdrawing 4 percent per year for spending (an amount deemed safe by traditional financial planning but warned about in my book, *The 4% Rule and Safe Withdrawal Rates*). **Even without inflation adjustments, you would wipe out 60 percent of your account just in spending alone.** When you add inflation, volatility drag, and investment losses to the equation, the overall destruction to equity would be the retirement equivalent of death by strangulation. It's why the sequence of returns risk defines the third side of our investment return triangle.

Conversely, now imagine the opposite situation where your portfolio grows for the first 15 years at 15 percent while you're only spending 4 percent (adjusted for inflation). Halfway through your 30-year retirement, you'll be richer than ever. You could stuff your money under a mattress, never make another dime, and still afford to live better than ever.

The surprising reality is every retiree is a market timer by birthright. Your sequence of returns is determined by your retirement date, which is a product of when you were born. It doesn't matter if your investment returns average out over the long run if your withdrawals in the first 10 years of retirement deplete a poorly performing portfolio.

An intuitive way to understand the problems caused by the combination of volatility drag and sequencing effects is to think of it as dollar-cost averaging[13] in reverse. You sell more shares to support the same amount of spending as the market declines, lowering your average sales price for any given fixed amount of spending. The greater the volatility and/or the worse the sequence of returns, the more dramatic the negative impact will be on your ability to spend money to support your lifestyle in retirement.

The counterintuitive conclusion is you shouldn't fear a sudden market crash at the start of your retirement. Instead, it's a prolonged flat market, or extended period of investment nonperformance, that should scare every retiree. Surprisingly, there's minimal relationship between your safe withdrawal rate in retirement and having the bad luck of starting your retirement in a bear market or even a market crash.

Quick market crashes don't cause irreparable damage because, over the short term, a conventional asset allocation portfolio rebalance would have you withdrawing needed cash to support spending from the bond allocation.

That's because the stocks declined in the bear market but the bonds likely didn't fall as much or possibly went up. Plus, over the short term, you're only withdrawing a few percent from your portfolio, which is not enough to cause a depletion problem. Assuming the market bounces back after the brief decline, your financial picture would still be intact.

The real risk is 10 years (notice the emphasis on that critically important 7 to 15-year time window again!) of portfolio nonperformance—what I call "flat spots." This is where your investments might experience a sudden decline, then a rise, and maybe some small up-and-down years. There is little net gain or loss to show for all that volatility at the end of those 10 years, yet your cumulative withdrawals could add up to a significant amount that has depleted your portfolio to an unrecoverable degree.

Worse yet, if you combine 10 years of investment nonperformance during your early retirement years with rising inflation, then the problems are multiplied because your portfolio gets depleted at an accelerated rate plus your total spending over your entire retirement lifespan is much higher than planned. For example, Michael Kitces at Kitces.com shows how a retiree who starts with nominal expenditures of $40,000 per year will spend $2.12 million over a 30-year retirement if 8 percent inflation occurs in the final 10 years. However, that retiree will need to spend a whopping $2.90 million if the same 8 percent inflation occurs in the first 10 years of retirement. That's an $800,000 increase—or 36 percent more total spending.

Putting this together, there are two significant risks that can dramatically affect how much money you need to retire:

1. The first risk is a 7 to 15-year period of investment nonperformance during the early phase of retirement resulting in such a substantial depletion of investment capital that the portfolio can't bounce back.

2. And the second risk is high inflation during the first phase of retirement, resulting in much higher spending than initially planned.

3. If you're particularly unfortunate and experience both of these risks together, then you'll face a particularly low safe withdrawal rate and will need to have an even bigger portfolio to support the same lifestyle.

This is not some strange, statistical mumbo-jumbo that has no bearing on your retirement. This is real-world stuff that is critical to your financial security. Real people retired in past decades with plans to spend 4 percent annually (adjusted for inflation) and were forced to rearrange their spending because of this exact problem. This is a critically important, real-world retirement planning problem that you must understand to secure your financial future.

Now can you see why a retirement plan based on the conventional assumption of long-term, historical average returns is so deceptively dangerous? The implication is that those average returns will just roll into your account year after year like clockwork when reality doesn't work that way at all. Investment returns ebb and flow, providing stellar results in one decade followed by bad results in another.

When you spend from your savings while your investments lose money, the resulting damage to your account value is magnified. It's a problem that every retiree faces. The following table illustrates the volatility effect and sequencing effect together by showing you how much your investment portfolio must return just to break even from any given loss, with no spending or spending 4 percent per year over a three-year period:

ILLUSTRATION 13

LOSS	% GAIN TO GET BACK TO EVEN	% GAIN TO GET BACK TO EVEN WITH 4% SPENDING
-10%	+11%	+26%
-20%	+25%	+42%
-30%	+43%	+63%
-50%	+100%	+132%

Notice how the spending magnifies losses in your investment portfolio and how hard it is to recover from those losses. *And this example is only showing a three-year impact.*

Remember, the real problem occurs from the perspective of a 7 to 15-year time period because a bad decade outlasts most cash reserve strategies, which leaves you eating away at your portfolio value until there's not enough left to recover. Spending from your portfolio adds insult to injury during periods of market adversity. It's why the order of returns is so terribly important and why volatility and inflation matter. A series of losses early in your retirement, combined with spending and/or inflation, can devastate a retirement plan.

Also, notice that this analysis only shows what it takes to break even (with and without spending), but it doesn't mention anything about growing your assets or offsetting inflation. When you add these two factors into the calculation, the problem is multiplied again.

The lesson here is that retirees really shouldn't worry about the short term because if a sudden bear market bounces back relatively quickly, the overall impact on a conventional asset allocation portfolio is not fatal. Conversely, conventional financial advice to focus on the long term (30 years or more) is equally misguided. What really matters is the intermediate term of 7 to 15 years. That first decade is what makes or breaks your financial security in retirement.

Fortunately, there's a solution because the sequence of returns risk isn't random. You can manage that risk.

CONNECTING ALL THREE SIDES TO FORM THE TRIANGLE

Now that we've defined the three sides of the investment return triangle, we can draw conclusions that impact how much money you need to retire. Here's what we know so far:

1. The sequence of returns dramatically affects how much you can safely spend from your savings.

2. Compound return is the only return you can spend, and it's always less than average return due to volatility drag.

3. Valuation-informed estimates for future investment return provide useful information not available from any other approach.

These are all essential facts to know about investment returns. Unfortunately, it's still not quite enough knowledge because our goal isn't to just gather interesting facts. You want to determine a reliable estimate for your investment return assumption, which is necessary to calculate how much money you need to retire. Your retirement security depends on that investment return estimate, which is the center of the triangle, but there are still questions remaining unanswered.

- For example, you still don't know where the negative sequence of returns risk is most likely to strike. Is it random, as some experts claim, or is there a way to reasonably estimate the risk of it hiding around the corner ready to hit you like a Mike Tyson punch?

- You also don't know when volatility is most likely to strike. Is it random, as experts claim, or is there a different explanation?

Fortunately, there are practical answers to both of these questions so you can effectively manage these risks in your retirement. Before we get to those, however, let's first look at the solution provided by traditional retirement planning to understand why that approach is more deceptive than instructive.

MONTE CARLO CALCULATORS AND OTHER "RANDOM" MYTHS

"THAT WHICH IS STATIC AND REPETITIVE IS BORING. THAT WHICH IS DYNAMIC AND RANDOM IS CONFUSING. IN BETWEEN LIES ART."

- JOHN LOCKE, ENGLISH PHILOSOPHER

Rob came to our first financial coaching session full of confidence. It was 2007, and the stock and real estate markets had been on the upswing for years, making him quite wealthy. He finally had enough money to retire after decades of working smart, saving diligently, and investing prudently.

Or at least that's what his financial advisor told him.

The only thing Rob wanted from our coaching relationship was to work on life fulfillment and planning issues for his dream retirement. He believed he had the financial part all worked out because his advisor's sophisticated Monte Carlo analysis looked scientifically accurate. It showed with 95 percent confidence that he had enough money to retire. Most financial planning clients in that situation feel the same blind confidence, and *that's the problem with Monte Carlo analysis.*

Our first coaching call didn't go as planned. I had to tell Rob that his financial planner failed to explain how a seemingly inconsequential 5 percent failure risk was a statistical concept that had limited applicability to his actual retirement. That 5 percent risk wasn't a random or unknowable factor. It was a conditional risk, and the bad news was that Rob had an uncomfortably high chance of being part of the 5 percent that failed due to the year he was retiring. His retirement wasn't nearly as secure as he was led to believe.

To say that Rob was shocked would be an understatement. Our coaching took a turn into the complex, dark recesses of Monte Carlo simulations, confidence intervals, and how seemingly small risks can show up in your life as a huge risk able to destroy your financial security.

The purpose of this chapter is to save you from being the next Rob.

Monte Carlo, the core algorithm behind most financial planning software, is the darling of the financial planning industry so you're absolutely going to encounter it as you plan for your retirement. You need to understand its limitations to make smart decisions.

Like all tools in retirement planning, it can provide value if used properly. Unfortunately, Monte Carlo calculators are highly sophisticated, statistical algorithms that aren't well understood by financial planning clients or many of the professionals who employ them. The result is widespread misuse and misinterpretation of the potentially valuable conclusions they can provide.

Be forewarned: I promise to keep everything as simple as possible to deliver useful conclusions about Monte Carlo with a minimum of complications, but this is sophisticated math and statistics. You must understand how it works for your own protection. The only choice, I'm sorry to say, is to just commit and dig in.

Monte Carlo Defined

Monte Carlo calculators are sophisticated computer programs that determine how random variation and lack of knowledge affects the reliability of a system. A Monte Carlo simulation is a stochastic process of iteratively evaluating a deterministic model by randomizing the inputs.

Yeah, I know…pretty hard to grasp in one read, right?

It's just fancy terminology for simulating sequences of random market returns into a confidence interval, which is a range of values that gives a specific probability outcome. Hmmm, if that still means nothing to you, don't worry because that's part of the problem with Monte Carlo analysis.

Monte Carlo simulations are useful for modeling uncertainty when an exact result using a deterministic model can't be attained. If the simulation is performed using financial and statistical expertise coupled with in-depth knowledge about the limitations inherent in the Monte Carlo process, then these models can provide useful insights. It's an incredibly powerful simulation tool that illuminates various aspects of randomness in retirement planning (such as investment return, inflation, or life expectancy) to show how financial plans perform in a wide variety of conditions. In the hands of a real expert, these programs bring greater understanding to the difficult task of modeling uncertainty than historical data alone can provide.

That's the positive part of this story. The problem is, it's not easy to get right.

How Monte Carlo Simulations Work

Monte Carlo simulations work by applying a random sampling of either actual historical data or simulated historical data to construct 30-year sequences of returns. When simulating returns, they assume multivariate normal or lognormal distributions with inputs based on an assumed mean, standard deviation, and correlation between each asset. (Yes, it's a mouthful.)

The result of all this fancy math is expressed simply as a percentage confidence interval—the number might be 30 percent, 85 percent, or even 100 percent— that your money lasted longer than your lifespan based on the assumptions applied. It means that if you had the assets and spending patterns specified in the model, you would have died before you spent all your money in that percentage of the simulations.

To make this more intuitive, let's look behind the curtain to see what's actually going on with these calculators. As it turns out, the whole "Monte Carlo magic" is really the same old retirement calculation like you can find anywhere online but with a simulation engine that varies certain input assumptions. This simulation engine allows the calculator to model thousands of potential future retirements by recalculating your same retirement over and over again with different assumptions. A certain number of these simulations have you run out of money before you die (failure), and a certain number of simulations have you die with money in the bank (success). The number of successes relative to the failures determines your confidence interval.

The important point is that it's the same old retirement calculation we've been discussing all along. There's nothing fundamentally new about the math. It's subject to the same assumption problems as any other conventional method. The only difference is that it varies the assumptions using fancy math and statistical rules.

Notice how this idea isn't really all that complicated once you understand it, but that's **not** how it presents to most future retirees. Instead, the façade of a scientific process coupled with a deceptively simple output number leads to false conclusions and misplaced confidence. It carries an extraordinarily high risk for misunderstanding because nonexperts, including seasoned financial planners, often misapply the math and data assumptions and/ or misinterpret the output so that the whole process deceives more than it enlightens. It's a serious problem for an otherwise useful tool.

Monte Carlo is widely considered the "rocket science" method of retirement calculators, but you must be careful. *It's still just a retirement calculator with limitations like all other retirement calculators.* Unfortunately, it's rarely presented that way to clients.

While Monte Carlo calculators have some advantages over more straightforward, deterministic calculators that simulate constant growth, that advantage comes at a cost.

THE PROBLEM WITH MONTE CARLO SOFTWARE

Monte Carlo assumes that the sequence of returns risk and volatility effects are random, but research proves they aren't. It also assumes correlations are stable, but research proves they aren't. It's a classic case of garbage in equals garbage out. *Any calculator that randomizes the return data or assumes stable correlations is misrepresenting reality.* That's a serious problem.

Monte Carlo's use in financial planning software is another example of brilliant mathematicians creating sophisticated financial models that are fundamentally flawed because they require assumptions that don't accurately represent the real world. When the assumptions are wrong, the mathematical projections are wrong, no matter how scientific the process may look. While the sequence of returns is not an entirely predictable assumption, research conclusively demonstrates that it's affected by market valuations at the beginning of your retirement. Monte Carlo hides that fact.

Sophisticated Monte Carlo practitioners claim these shortcomings are manageable by adjusting the expected return and standard deviation assumptions, but that contradicts the entire premise of Monte Carlo—that returns are random, not deterministic. If changing return assumptions is the solution, then there's no point in bothering with all the statistical complexity of Monte Carlo in the first place because it can be done with more straightforward, intuitive calculators.

For example, retirement calculators using historical US stock market data would tell you the 4 percent rule (also known as the safe withdraw rate) had a 95 percent success rate. That means your money lasted 30 years or longer 95 percent of the time, but 5 percent of the time you ran out of money before the 30-year period ended. A Monte Carlo calculator would give you similar confidence intervals depending on the chosen assumptions. Nothing new.

How to Interpret Monte Carlo Results

Like Rob, most people would conclude a 95 percent confidence interval is safe enough. After all, only one out of every 20 situations failed. Those are pretty good odds, but they're oversimplified.

For example, most people experience a *1 in 20 risk of failure* as sounding more dangerous than a *95 percent chance of success*, even though they're the exact same thing. Even the terms "failure" and "success" are vague. Does it mean you run out of money before you die? Or does it mean you overspent for the first four years, so you need to slightly adjust your spending on a walk-forward basis? Do you really know how to apply that confidence interval to your financial life?

These differences in interpretation are game-changing, but they're seldom understood or explained. Worse yet, because the Monte Carlo simulation randomizes all data, it completely misses the most crucial fact of all: *The failures aren't random!!* Risk is not equally distributed but instead clusters around 30-year periods that begin with the highest valuations. That means if you're in a similar valuation period, you should feel fear instead of the false hope implied by a 95 percent Monte Carlo confidence interval.

Sequence of Returns Risk Isn't Random

There's a rule of thumb that many financial planners use to help their clients calculate how much money they need to retire and what amount they can spend each year. In the industry it's called "the 4 percent rule."

A lot of factors can impact this "rule." Ed Easterling of Crestmont Research brilliantly revealed the connection between market valuations, sequence of returns risk, and retirement spending rules when he tested the industry-standard 4 percent rule against all 30-year periods in stock market history (S&P 500 Index including dividends) beginning in 1900. He ranked each 30-year period by market valuation as determined by the price/earnings ratio on the first year of retirement, then organized those data periods into 4 separate quartiles[14] of market valuation, from highest to lowest.

ILLUSTRATION 14

SAFE WITHDRAWAL STATISTICS BY P/E QUARTILES

4 percent SWR 30-Year Periods Since 1900 Starting Account Value = $1,000,000   [Data courtesy of CrestmontResearch.Com]

STARTING QUARTILES	P/E RANGE	SUCCESS RATE	AVERAGE ENDING $$	AVERAGE YRS IF FAILURE
TOP 25%	18.5+	79%	$2,787,045	27.3
SECOND 25%	13.9 TO 18.4	100%	$5,157,631	N/A
THIRD 25%	11.2 TO 13.8	100%	$8,613,308	N/A
BOTTOM 25%	BELOW 11.2	100%	$10,073,325	N/A
ALL PERIODS	14.6 AVG	95% AVG	$6,663,664	27.3

Look at that table closely. Notice how all the failures began with market valuations in the highest 25 percent grouping. Every single failure without exception started with a stock market P/E above 18.5. It's not random, and that's an essential fact to understand for your investment return assumption when estimating how much money you need to retire.

Stated another way, the failure risk was 1 in 20 for a "95 percent confidence interval" for all of the 30-year data periods. The failure risk for the highest valued quartile was more substantial at 1 in 5, while the failure risk for the lowest valued quartile was zero. That's a huge difference.

Worse yet, these numbers **understate the real difference in risk** because there's something that's not apparent on the surface. Many high valuation periods that "succeeded" did so by barely staying above zero. I guarantee your retirement won't feel like a success if you end up in that situation. Instead, you would experience it as failure because you would radically reduce your lifestyle and live in fear of going broke, even if your assets never made it all the way to zero. When your account balances get uncomfortably low, your natural response will be to cut back your spending dramatically to try and remain financially solvent. When you count these "near misses" as actual failures, the risk difference becomes even more dramatic. *Your confidence will justifiably be replaced by concern.*

Market valuation at the beginning of your retirement is a highly significant indicator of your risk of financial failure during retirement. Valuation is a useful tool for identifying the highest risk of failure because that risk is not random as both backcasting and Monte Carlo simulations would imply.

VALUATION MATTERS TO YOU BUT NOT MONTE CARLO

Also, notice how the above table shows a direct relationship between market valuations at the time you began retirement and the average ending balance in your account. The lower the market valuation, the higher your average ending savings balance after 30 years of spending. The higher the market valuation at the beginning of retirement, the lower your average ending savings balance.

Some critics might claim this example is too neat and tidy—possibly the result of data mining. It's not, and to prove the point, we'll now increase the spending rate to 5 percent (instead of the previous 4 percent). This will demonstrate the progressive increase in risk across valuation quartiles.

ILLUSTRATION 15

SAFE WITHDRAWAL STATISTICS BY P/E QUARTILES

5 Percent SWR 30-Year Periods Since 1900 Starting Account Value =
$1,000,000   [Data courtesy of CrestmontResearch.Com]

STARTING QUARTILES	P/E RANGE	SUCCESS RATE	AVERAGE ENDING $$	AVERAGE YRS IF FAILURE
TOP 25%	18.5+	47%	$(850,676)	21.8
SECOND 25%	13.9 TO 18.4	70%	$1,607,294	21.5
THIRD 25%	11.2 TO 13.8	80%	$6,326,247	26.5
BOTTOM 25%	BELOW 11.2	95%	$7,661,859	30.0
ALL PERIODS	14.6 AVG	73% AVG	$3,693,376	23.0

Notice how the average success rate has dropped to 73 percent because of the higher spending rate—in other words, the odds are roughly 3 out of 4 that you will not run out of money before you run out of life. Surprisingly, higher withdrawal rates are successful in the overwhelming majority of 30-year periods with the failures highly concentrated in the most overvalued periods. The 30-year periods beginning with the top valuation quartile saw more than a 50 percent failure rate—1 out of every 2. That's pretty dangerous. The bottom valuation period was much safer with a 95 percent success rate in supporting a withdrawal that was 20 percent higher (5 percent instead of 4 percent).

The Monte Carlo and backcasting approaches completely miss the importance of market valuation in assessing retirement failure risk. They assume investment return is random and has no relationship to any factor that can be known when you begin retirement. *This assumption is not supported by the data.* They treat your retirement like a crapshoot when it isn't. You can absolutely know with 100 percent certainty the stock market valuations and interest rates at the beginning of your retirement. This knowledge changes your odds of success or failure dramatically.

THE 10 MOST IMPORTANT THINGS TO KNOW ABOUT MONTE CARLO CALCULATORS

If your financial advisor is using Monte Carlo analysis, then make sure you carefully consider the following issues:

1. Remember that a 75 percent confidence interval sounds impressive, but it implies 25 percent of the time the strategy failed on simulated results. That is 1 in 4. The problem with confidence intervals is they lull you into false confidence. Your retirement will produce a binary result, not an average result. You'll either be 100 percent in the failure group or 100 percent in the successful group. No individual can ever experience a probabilistic outcome for the same reason you

can't be 73 percent dead at age 82. Probabilities deceive for individual outcomes, so beware.

2. Monte Carlo may attempt to predict the risk of failure, but it tells you nothing about the cause of risk so you can protect your portfolio. This issue is critical because research shows that risk is associated with market valuations. Randomizing returns obscures that fact, making it more challenging to know how to protect yourself.

3. Monte Carlo simulators do a poor job of telling you the risk of unlikely events that occur with alarming frequency, such as the 1987 stock market crash, the 2001 to 2002 bear market or the 2008 to 2009 Great Recession. Research shows these events are associated with declining markets following periods of overvaluation. Only valuation-based models provide any useful indication when volatility risks are highest.

4. Monte Carlo analysis cannot include the portfolio diversification benefits of nontraditional assets such as owning your own business or rental real estate. It makes the expedient assumption that your portfolio is composed of the stocks, bonds, and mutual funds (paper assets) that your financial advisor can sell you, which may have little relevance to your specific investment strategy or actual asset composition. Changing your portfolio composition to include alternative

assets and investment strategies changes your risk dramatically.

5. If you try to model more complex portfolios than the conventional 60 percent stock/40 percent bond portfolio, then correlation assumptions become unrealistically complex as the number of asset classes increase. It makes the correlations difficult, if not impossible, to accurately model. This is critically important because if you fail to model the correlations, the software still requires that assumption to crunch the numbers. As a result, it will likely assume a correlation of zero when actual correlations are usually much, much higher thus understating true risk. Not only that, but correlations vary across time. Long-term correlation data masks the intensely increased periods of high correlation that occur during bear markets. Correlation assumptions are a serious problem in Monte Carlo analysis, which can cause it to overstate the value of diversification and potentially understate risk.

6. Monte Carlo ignores the relationship between market fundamentals and subsequent investment returns, otherwise known as "regime" based returns. The software, by necessity, assumes all data periods should be treated equally, even though actual data shows market returns, correlations, and volatility vary widely in different regimes. The most relevant periods for analysis are those

with the most similar conditions. If market valuations are above average at the time you retire, then you'll want to consider data from those periods and not be unduly swayed by the higher investment returns that followed below-average valuation periods. Rising interest rate regimes are different from declining interest rates. The expected returns, correlation, and volatility are entirely different in bull markets versus bear markets. High valuation periods versus low valuation, or high inflation versus low inflation, all produce very different market data. You can't use a single data set and assume it's universally applicable across varying market conditions; yet, to the best of my knowledge, no Monte Carlo software can accurately model all of these varying conditions.

7.   Monte Carlo randomizes return data, which is inconsistent with the secular trends that naturally occur in real market history. The markets are admittedly random in the short term but exhibit trends over extended periods. These trends cause meaningful periods of above and below-average returns that are extremely important to real-world retirees, as evidenced by the sequence of returns risk. This vital information is obscured by the randomizing nature of Monte Carlo sampling.

8.   Monte Carlo does not reflect human nature. It assumes spending patterns will remain fixed according to an algorithm. But real-world retirees

increase spending when their assets grow and decrease spending when their assets decline in value. This change in spending behavior can have a more substantial impact on the risk of financial failure than the data sampling produced by Monte Carlo would imply, but it's excluded from the analysis.

9. Monte Carlo software forces the user to choose a specific type of investment return distribution to run its calculations—normal, log-normal, triangular, binomial, exponential, etc. However, the data proves return distributions vary over time. There is no best single answer to distributions, yet one must be chosen for the program to function.

10. Monte Carlo programs provide output that implies a complete assessment of retirement failure risk, but the truth is most free applications and many paid Monte Carlo applications measure only one type of risk faced by future retirees—investment return risk. Some versions may model other types of risk (longevity, inflation, healthcare costs, etc.), but the output usually doesn't communicate these various risks and their impact on retirement planning in a way that the user can act on.

The bottom line is that Monte Carlo calculators are useful tools, but their value is limited. They do a perfectly adequate job of letting you know if your retirement plan is broadly on track, but so do more straightforward calculation methods that are intuitive to understand.

Monte Carlo also has the advantage of illustrating specific aspects of retirement planning that are impossible to model any other way. If used correctly and understood well, those simulations can provide some limited value for practical application. If not managed properly, there is a real risk of misinformation.

The reality is Monte Carlo calculators face the same limitations of every other type of retirement calculator, but it's wrapped in a sophisticated package that is harder for most retirees to accurately work with. When you look under the hood, you'll find it's still just a mathematical projection of assumptions. That means the accuracy of the calculated projection remains 100 percent dependent on how closely the assumptions align with future reality. And as you learned above, those assumptions are not close enough to reality to bet your financial future on.

If you'd like an alternative, I provide a practical set of solutions with my free Ultimate Retirement Calculator (https://financialmentor.com/retirement-calculator) and the accompanying paid mini-course explaining how to use it (https://financialmentor.com/calculator-course). You'll discover a more straightforward, intuitive way to model the sequence of returns risk and different expected returns based on valuation. Best of all, everything remains 100 percent in your control.

HOW VALUATIONS MAKE OR BREAK YOUR RETIREMENT

"THE ONLY FUNCTION OF ECONOMIC FORECASTING IS TO MAKE ASTROLOGY LOOK RESPECTABLE."

- JOHN KENNETH GALBRAITH, ECONOMIST

When Pat divorced in 1983, she had two teenage children, a mortgage, few assets, and the sole responsibility of securing her financial future. Not an easy task, but fortunately she was well educated and had a stable career.

When she read how stocks outperform other assets over the long term, she decided to bet all of her savings and retirement plan funds on the stock market. Luck was on her side. By the time February 2000 rolled around, Pat was finalizing her upcoming retirement with a fat savings balance and retirement accounts bolstered by one of the greatest bull markets in history.

She was a brilliantly lucky *market timer by birthright*, having ridden the rising tide of the stock market all the way up until she retired at the very top.

Pat had two other advantages. She was working with

me in 1999 and had a competent financial advisor who understood the importance of market valuations on risk and reward. We both convinced her to reallocate the bulk of her assets to rental real estate and bonds to reduce risk and prepare her finances for the next stage of her life. When the devastating bear market came months later, she hardly blinked. Her financial security had been saved.

Unfortunately, Greg wasn't so lucky. He was part of the Silicon Valley technology start-up scene and bought the story that you should invest in what you know and understand. Greg's passion was all things technology, and fortunately for Greg, the late 1990s was a fantastic time to invest in technology. The internet dotcom bubble was full-blown, and the few companies that actually had earnings were selling at ridiculous valuations. Everyone investing in tech was making a fortune, and Greg's entire portfolio was a cliché of big-name dot-com stocks. He was rich.

By the time we started working together, Greg was a confident new retiree, and the entire NASDAQ index, comprised mostly of tech stocks, was selling for more than 200 times earnings. Greg confused brains with a bull market by thinking he was a brilliant investor. Unfortunately, he had just gotten lucky by being in the right place, at the right time, with the right strategy. According to market valuations, the risk was extraordinarily high that his luck was about to run out.

I tried to teach him about risk management and help him see the downside potential of such lofty investment valuations. He wanted nothing to do with it and fired me as his financial coach. Within months, the subsequent bear market decline reduced his net worth by more than 80 percent. He went back to work.

Investment return analyses that fail to account for market valuation and interest rates provide no useful information for estimating your risk profile and expected return over the critical first 7 to 15 years of your retirement. Research proves that your investment performance during this time window will make or break your financial security in retirement. It's critically important that you know how to manage it.

For example, nobody relying on any of the popular backcasting or Monte Carlo calculators could have anticipated the high-risk, low-return investment environment beginning in 2000 or 2008. However, subsequent investment returns were life-changing for Greg and many other new retirees at that time. Only valuation-based models provided early warning information to help you manage the risk.

That's why valuation metrics at the beginning of your retirement are a superior modeling tool. They are the only investment return modeling approach that gives you useful information for your actual retirement time horizon. Wade Pfau, Professor of retirement income at the American College (https://bit.ly/2Mv929W), has shown that retirement success is highly dependent upon early investment returns. His research shows that remaining wealth after 10 years of retirement, combined with cumulative inflation over that period, explains 80 percent of the variation in the amount you can safely withdraw from savings.

In his May 2008 report, Michael Kitces (http://bit.ly/31IZH0x) used 140 years of data to demonstrate that the safe withdrawal rate for a 30-year retirement is 0.91 correlated to the annualized real investment return over the first 15 years of retirement. Correlation measures the relationship or connection between two variables showing how one thing affects another. It's quantified as a range with 1 being perfectly related, -1 being a perfect inverse relationship, and 0 having no relationship at all. That makes 0.91 an astoundingly tight relationship between the first 15 years of real investment return and your safe withdrawal rate in retirement. Additionally, Kitces' conclusion is consistent with the research by Pfau, Bernstein, and Easterling, among others; it's not an anomaly.

When real investment returns were elevated in the first 15 years of retirement, significantly higher withdrawal rates could be sustained. Conversely, when real returns were depressed for the first 15 years of retirement, lower safe withdrawal rates were the likely result. For every instance where the safe withdrawal rate was below 6 percent, the first 15 years also provided a below-average real investment return of just 4 percent or less.

Market valuations at the time you begin your investment holding period are inversely correlated to the return you can expect over the next 7 to 15 years. In fact, Kitces showed the inverse correlation between investment performance and valuation from 1871 to 2005 was an impressive -0.65. This issue has been well researched and is valid across both international and domestic historical data samples. In other words, it's reliable enough to apply in your own retirement planning.

CONNECTING VALUATION TO YOUR INVESTMENT RETURN TRIANGLE

Putting the sides of the investment return triangle together, one side tells us investment returns are related to market valuations, and the other two sides tell us the first 15 years of investment returns will make or break your financial security in retirement. Given that, is market valuation at the beginning of retirement a reasonable measure of financial success during retirement?

As it turns out, the answer is "yes," with a strong negative correlation of -0.74.

Low valuations at the beginning of retirement indicate higher safe withdrawal rates and total investment return over the subsequent 30-year retirement. The converse is also true where high market valuations indicate lower safe withdrawal rates and lower investment returns. This is demonstrated by research from both Easterling and Kitces. This provides critical information for estimating your expected investment return when calculating how much money you need to retire.

SAFE WITHDRAWAL RATES BASED ON P/E 10 QUINTILES

(DATA COURTESY OF CRESTMONTRESEARCH.COM)

QUINTILE	LOWER P/E	UPPER P/E	LOWEST SWR	HIGHEST SWR	AVERAGE SWR
1	5.4	12.0	5.7 %	10.6 %	8.1 %
2	12.0	14.7	4.8 %	8.3 %	6.7 %
3	14.7	17.6	4.9 %	8.1 %	6.3 %
4	17.6	19.9	4.9 %	7.2 %	5.8 %
5	19.9	28.7	4.4 %	6.1 %	5.1 %

Notice how the impact of market valuation is most pronounced at the extremes.

Your best-case scenario from overvalued markets is almost the same as your worst-case scenario from favorably valued markets. The average safe withdrawal rate varies by an astonishing 3 percent from top to bottom. That may not sound like much, but it would literally increase the amount of money you can safely spend each month during retirement by 60 percent or more. Obviously, that's a big deal.

Wade Pfau (http://bit.ly/31NJBme) came to conceptually similar conclusions by creating a robust model for predicting the amount a retiree could safely withdraw from savings using regression analysis and three valuation metrics: P/E 10 (price divided by average real earnings for previous 10 years), dividend yield (dividends divided by stock price), and interest rates (on 10-year government bonds). It wasn't perfect, but most of the calculations were within 1 percent of accurately forecasting how much money you could safely spend from your portfolio in retirement. That's far more accurate and informative than blindly following historical averages or betting on random Monte Carlo results.

The research is clear—valuation matters. It's a valid indicator for narrowing the range of investment return results to consider when estimating the money you need to retire.

I know this was a lot of information to digest to get to this point, but I hope you see that the value of the conclusion was well worth the price. It's diametrically opposed to the conventional wisdom of Monte Carlo calculators, average returns, and assumptions of randomness that you'll find elsewhere. This is shocking because it's fully supported by the research and is so important that it results in life-changing conclusions for your retirement planning.

The Valuation Approach to Estimate Your Retirement Needs

The way you apply the valuation approach to your plan is to examine market valuations today and compare them to the tables provided earlier in this book. This will not tell you what your expected investment returns will be, but it will indicate if the time is high risk or low risk so you know if you can reasonably expect better-than-average or worse-than-average results.

- Complete your calculations using my retirement calculator, which allows you to control the investment return assumption. (https://financial mentor.com/retirement-calculator). Use historical averages as a reasonable assumption for the long-term estimate, then adjust the intermediate-term investment returns to properly model sequence of returns risk and lower (or higher) expected returns. The Ultimate Retirement Calculator has extra, built-in features that allow you to model those situations easily and accurately.

- Don't assume investment returns below fixed income (bonds) because you could always lock in fixed income returns, annuities, and/or purchase TIPs as a no-brainer alternative.

- Only assume returns above long-term historical averages if you have a nontraditional portfolio and demonstrated investment experience to support higher return expectations, or the markets are significantly below historical average valuations (see risk profile from the first step).

- Separate your portfolio into nontraditional and traditional asset classes before developing your expected return analysis. They are such different animals that they require different models and assumptions. The upper half of my Ultimate Retirement Calculator is perfect for modeling a traditional asset allocation portfolio. The lower half is designed for modeling nontraditional assets like business or rental real estate so they all fit within a single, composite calculation.

I would not recommend backcasting or Monte Carlo-type calculators because they aren't easily adapted to balance long-term average returns with intermediate-term sequence risk. Plus, they don't model alternative assets in the same portfolio as conventional asset allocation, which you need to accurately estimate how much you need to retire.

Most calculators aren't able to build models that show investment returns and sequence of returns risk are related to valuations at the beginning of your retirement. And if you find a calculator that can, then it usually can't model a modern retirement plan that includes other asset classes like business and rental real estate. If your retirement plan is impacted by all the above, then your retirement model must include all the above.

INVESTMENT RETURN MODELING LIMITATIONS

I'm not claiming you can accurately predict your investment return using valuation approaches, particularly in the short term. You can't. You'll never know in advance what your actual investment returns will be or the exact sequence of returns.

However, expectancy models based on valuation provide a superior solution to any other alternative. It's the only method that provides any useful indication of the risk and reward profile you face during the critical first 7 to 15 years of your actual retirement. That's why I recommend this approach exclusively.

The truth is that your investment returns won't be totally random, nor will they be representative of all periods in history. Instead, it's wiser to assume your returns will relate in some way to the most representative sample of history—the periods that match the market valuations you face on the day you retire.

Writing in his 2008 book, *Enough,* John Bogle, founder of Vanguard funds, made a similar point.

> *"My concern is that too many of us make the implicit assumption that stock market history repeats itself when we know, deep down, that the only valid prism through which to view the market's future is the one that takes into account not history, but the sources of stock returns."*

The stock market's long-term source of return is dividends and growth, but over the short-to-intermediate term (1 to 15 years), returns can be dominated by changes in market valuation. It's the tail that wags the dog, and research has shown how today's interest rates and market valuation are connected to how that tail wags in the future.

As this book goes to press in the final quarter of 2019, the US financial markets are in uncharted territory with a rare combination of both record high stock market valuation for equities and record low interest rates for the credit markets (bonds, money market funds). Blind simulations based on history can't analyze those risks properly, which is why it's imperative to follow Jack Bogle's wisdom by using models that will adjust for these changes.

That said, financial modeling is always a probabilistic outcome, at best. There's always uncertainty, which is why you'll be learning how to simulate confidence intervals in the pages that follow. Expectancy models based on current valuation and interest rates simply help to define that range of high and low estimates better than any other approach. That's why they're essential to your retirement plan.

PART 5

HOW TO ESTIMATE YOUR "MAGICAL" RETIREMENT NUMBER

"RETIREMENT PLANNING IS COMPLEX, PRONE TO LARGE ERRORS IN ESTIMATION, AND SHOULD EMBODY A LARGE MARGIN OF ERROR."

- WILLIAM BENGEN, CREATOR OF THE 4 PERCENT RULE

SIMPLE MODELS TO CALCULATE YOUR MAGIC NUMBER

Congratulations! That was a lot to cover. But now you're armed with the information you need to accurately plan a financially secure retirement.

The most important points to take away from the first half of this book are:

- **Conventional retirement planning is not working** for most people. The average worker lacks the skills and knowledge to successfully convert that model into a secure financial future.

- Conventional retirement planning is nothing more than a mathematical projection of assumptions into the future. **Your actual results will only be as accurate as the assumptions** used to create the plan.

- The assumptions required by the traditional retirement planning model are **unknowable** and out of your control, including the age you'll die, how healthy you'll be in your final years, and the national inflation rate between now and then.

- The conventional solution is to **assume average numbers for these required inputs, but this is a fundamentally flawed approach** because your life is a sample size of one. How long you live and what investment returns and inflation you experience have no causal relationship to statistical averages.

- Even if you accurately guessed the national inflation rate for 30 years into the future, your personal inflation may show little relation to the statistical inflation rate because where you live and what you buy may be totally different than the national average.

- The conventional plan assumes **you invest exclusively in a passive asset allocation** portfolio made up of the stocks, bonds, and mutual funds your financial planner can sell you. If your actual portfolio includes alternative assets like active investing strategies, directly owned rental real estate, or business entrepreneurship, your numbers will look very different. Unfortunately, most retirement calculators can't handle these alternative investments even though they're relatively common.

- The favored retirement calculator solution in the financial planning profession is **the Monte Carlo Calculator, which has serious limitations**.

- All retirement calculators, including Monte Carlo, have similar limitations since they use the same input numbers to perform the same calculation. The only difference is how they apply the required assumptions and represent the output.

- Accuracy is a matter of which assumptions you choose, not which calculator you choose. *That's why this book so far has focused on explaining the nuances of retirement planning assumptions.* That's what will make or break the accuracy of your plan. It's the required foundational knowledge necessary to apply the solutions in the second half of this book.

- Investment performance is one of the most complex and important assumptions. **The final 7 to 15 years of investment performance *before* you retire is one of the key determinants of the size of your nest egg, and the first 7 to 15**

years of investment performance *after* **you retire is one of the key determinants of how much you can safely spend from that nest egg.** That means you don't have the long-term horizon advocated by conventional financial planning, but instead, you have a series of intermediate-term investment horizons, each critical to your financial outcome in life. One determines your ending wealth, and the other determines how much you can spend from that wealth.

- Market valuation at the beginning of each 7 to 15-year period demonstrates a clear relationship to subsequent returns. Understanding that principle alone can change how you approach retirement when you get there.

- A smart way to **reduce the assumption risk built into retirement calculator projections is to iterate your plan on a walk-forward basis** during retirement. When you replace assumed data with actual data every few years during retirement, you will reduce the compound effect of small assumption errors growing into large financial problems.

- Despite the obvious shortcomings in the conventional retirement model, **it still has value.** You can use it to set target goals that result in meaningful action toward those goals.

Plus, it teaches critically important principles about retirement planning that, in combination with two other models taught here, you'll use to secure your financial future.

Now that you understand these key points, it's time to begin estimating your retirement number.

THE DIVIDEND DISCOUNT MODEL EXPLAINED

The first model you're going to apply is also one of the simplest. I call it the Dividend Discount Model (DDM) because of how the math is analogous to the dividend discount models used in stock price valuation. Despite the sophisticated sounding name, it's crazy simple to use. We'll start by first defining what it is and how it works.

The Dividend Discount Model is rooted in the financial concept that the value of any asset is the discounted present value of its cash flows. For the real estate asset class, that theory gets applied in formulas like the Capitalization Rate[15] and Gross Rent Multiplier[16] that determine real estate values as a multiple of either their net or gross rental income.

Similarly, the Dividend Discount Model was developed to show how the value of a stock is related to the net present value of its estimated future dividend income. The theory is that a stock's intrinsic value is the sum total of all the future cash flows that it will pay, discounted back to their present value.

The reason it's such a useful parallel in retirement planning is that the amount of money you need to retire works the same way—it's the sum total of all the future payments you need to support spending, discounted back to their present value.

In the example that follows, your task is to replace my hypothetical numbers with your actual assumption estimates so you develop your personalized retirement estimate. If you haven't created a set of assumptions for any of the questions, then please complete those estimates now before continuing. You'll get far more value out of the examples in this book when you can follow along with a pencil and paper using your own numbers so it's personal versus theoretical.

If you haven't yet had a chance to claim your free downloadable workbook so you have printable spreadsheets for each model, please go now to https://financial mentor.com/free-stuff/retirement-book. It makes everything fill-in-the-blank simple.

THE DIVIDEND DISCOUNT MODEL APPLIED

The first step in calculating your retirement number is to guesstimate your required income. Remember, conventional wisdom says you need 75 to 85 percent of your preretirement earnings in the first year of retirement.

For my hypothetical example, I'll use $100,000 just to keep the math easy. You can use your actual first-year estimate of your projected retirement spending. It's important to note this is only a first-year spending estimate. If you've planned for wildly varying spending patterns over time in your retirement, then just pick a representative estimate for the first year.

Next, subtract pension and social security income to determine a net income shortfall to be pulled from savings. Again, please use your actual numbers while I keep the math simple in this demonstration by assuming two spouses will receive combined social security totaling $30,000 annually and a small pension paying $20,000 annually. This totals $50,000 per year in income, leaving an annual shortfall of $50,000 that must be covered by savings ($100,000 total income - $50,000 social security and pension = $50,000 annual income shortfall).

Notice that we have so far ignored taxes to keep the math simple. If that bothers you, then go ahead and work with net numbers to increase accuracy. For example, if I was paying an effective combined state and federal tax rate of 25 percent and I need $100,000 of income, I could work with $133,000 of gross income (100,000/(1 - 0.25)). I'll stay with the $100,000 number because I want to keep the focus on principles, not mathematics, but feel free to decide what's best for you.

The next step is to convert the income shortfall into an asset savings requirement using the Dividend Discount Model. In other words, you'll compute how much money you need to save to provide $50,000 per year in additional spending during retirement. In my hypothetical example the income shortfall is $50,000, but you can use your actual numbers.

To calculate the amount of traditional savings you need to support paying $50,000 per year while adjusting for inflation, divide the income required by your expected return on investment minus inflation. In this example, let's apply traditional finance assumptions with assets earning 8 percent and inflation at 3 percent, giving you an after-inflation adjusted return of 5 percent (8 percent - 3 percent = 5 percent). Divide $50,000 by 0.05 (5 percent), and the magic number is $1,000,000 in retirement savings.

What that means is someone who wants to spend $100,000 per year in retirement when inflation averages 3 percent and nominal asset returns average 8 percent will need approximately $1,000,000 in savings. That assumes they get $50,000 per year income in real terms (inflation adjusted) from both social security and pensions over their remaining lifetime. Whew, that is a mouthful, not to mention a lot of assumptions.

Remember, this is just one estimate using one retirement planning model with one set of assumptions. It's not scripture-in-stone reality. Instead, it's a loose approximation that puts you somewhere in the ballpark, but only if your assumptions also are somewhere in the ballpark. If you used an online retirement calculator to check the accuracy and got wildly different numbers, then check your assumptions. Remember, it's never about the calculator but always about the assumptions.

That's why the next step in this process is to build a confidence interval by varying your critical assumptions over a plausible range. A confidence interval shows you how the amount of savings required varies as you change the assumptions. *You also need to identify which assumptions are critical to your retirement estimate and will have the most significant impact when changed. Focus on monitoring those carefully as you walk forward your estimate throughout your retirement.* Finally, you want to gauge the stability of your estimate so you can retire with confidence and security, knowing that you won't run out of money.

BUILDING CONFIDENCE INTO YOUR PLAN

"MODELS ARE TO BE USED, NOT BELIEVED."

- H. THEIL, DUTCH ECONOMETRICIAN

How can you confidently know that your future is financially secure when the model you're using to answer that question is built on assumptions about that future you can't possibly know with confidence?

One solution is that you recalculate your retirement plan every few years by replacing assumption data with actual data as discussed earlier. Each time you recalculate your plan and make adjustments as necessary, the amount of potential error is reduced.

Another solution is to build a confidence interval by varying each of your model input assumptions across the full range of what's reasonably plausible. You start with the most optimistic estimates (defined as easiest to achieve, resulting in the lowest savings estimate) and move to the most conservative estimates (defined as hardest to achieve, resulting in the highest savings requirement). The resulting output gives you a range of estimates for how much money you need to retire, varying from low to high, so you can see where your net worth fits into that range. The closer your retirement assets are to the upper end of your confidence interval, the more confident and conservative you can feel about your retirement planning.

Using the earlier example, let's apply conservative estimates by cutting my pension and social security in half so that my combined income sources provide just $15,000 per year instead of $50,000. This $35,000 annual reduction in pension income means the amount of income from savings must correspondingly rise by $35,000 to $85,000. If all else remains the same, my example retirement savings number rises to $1.7 million (an annual income shortfall of $85,000 divided by 0.05).

I can further stress-test this same scenario by conservatively assuming my investment return falls to 6 percent and inflation rises to 4 percent. That reduces my real investment return assumption to just 2 percent (6 percent return minus 4 percent inflation equals 2 percent or 0.02). Yikes, now my savings requirement for the same $100,000 annual income rises all the way to $4.25 million ($85,000 divided by 0.02 equals $4.25 million).

Notice how wide the range of values for my example retirement savings has grown to: one million dollars to $4.25 million. That's why I've claimed all along that there's no such thing as a magical retirement number that tells you exactly how much you need to retire. It all depends on your assumptions.

No single assumption has a prayer of being accurate for

30 to 50 years into the future. That's why you want to test a range of plausible outcomes. When you combine all of the pessimistic assumptions together (e.g., high inflation and low investment return) into a single calculation, it creates a huge retirement savings number. When you group the optimistic numbers together, your savings requirement is only fractionally as large. The effect is multiplicative (not additive), causing a shockingly wide range of perfectly plausible outcomes.

Do I Really Need a Confidence Interval?

Some people might claim the four million dollar number is overkill. After all, the goal was to spend $100,000 per year, and $4.25 million allows you to spend $100,000 for 42 years (without adjusting for inflation) even if your assets never earned a dime. There's good reason to believe it might be a conservative estimate, but we really don't know. After 42 years of inflation, $100,000 per year may not buy very much. You also don't know how your investments will perform, how long you'll live, or what unexpected expenses and medical problems might occur along the way.

The truth is that we can find valid criticisms for every retirement model, regardless of its sophistication. For example, careful readers will notice this model cannot adjust for sequence of returns risk. That is a definite negative. You'll have to build that risk into your expected return by lowering your estimates as a best approximation or use smarter alternatives that are more accurate. (See the *Retirement Calculator Secrets* mini-course for details at https://financialmentor.com/calculator-course.)

Despite that limitation, I chose to start with the dividend discount model because it has many qualities making it worthy of consideration. First, it assumes you don't spend principal, implying an infinite lifetime so you don't have to worry about outliving your assets. Did you notice that we ignored the life expectancy assumption when doing the calculations above? This greatly simplifies the math and gets rid of one significant risk.

Another advantage is that it's flexible. You can easily adjust return assumptions to include nontraditional assets. Other benefits of this model include that it does a reasonable job of adjusting for inflation and, most important, *it's easy to calculate—anyone can do it.*

In fact, you're going to prove how easy it is by calculating your confidence interval using your actual numbers right now. Don't worry about accuracy; just use your best guess for your personal assumptions and get comfortable with the calculations. It's a simple four-step process using basic math.

(See the table below for a template using our earlier example. Or better yet, get a fill-in-the-blank printable workbook that includes this template at https://financial mentor.com/free-stuff/retirement-book.)

BUILD YOUR CONFIDENCE INTERVAL STEP-BY-STEP

Start with the amount of income you require during retirement. In our example, it was $100,000 (Step A). Then subtract the amount of income you expect annually from social security and pensions (Step B). Divide what remains by your assumptions for investment returns minus inflation (Steps C & D). The result is the amount of savings you would require to retire with security and meet your income needs in perpetuity.

BUILD YOUR CONFIDENCE INTERVAL STEP-BY-STEP

	Optimistic	Expected	Conservative
Step A: Retirement Income Needs	$100,000	$100,000	$100,000
Step B: Social Security + Pension	$60,000	$50,000	$15,000
Step C: Investment Return – Inflation	.09-.02=.07	.08-.03=.05	.06-.04=.02
Step D: [A-B]/C = Total Savings	$571,000	$1,000,000	$4,250,000

Here are some additional tips to help you build your confidence interval when completing this exercise:

- Round your assumptions to the nearest $5,000 or $10,000 to keep the math simple, similar to what I did in the example.

- Make sure to play with various assumptions to find your range. The math is so simple you can vary each assumption with minimal effort and run a test case. Using multiple assumptions, you should have 20 or more test cases when you're done.

- Try adjusting your income needs to include taxes.

- Try adjusting your net investment return based on current market valuations.

- Make sure one extreme of your interval includes all your best-case assumptions, and the other includes all your worst-case assumptions, including adjusting for taxes.

Completing this exercise using real numbers from your life is important because you'll get far more value out of the remaining chapters. Everything that follows builds on this exercise, so I encourage you to spend 10 minutes completing the process before continuing. Even if you're math-phobic, the calculations are so simple that there's no reason not to get it done.

When you're finished modeling, you'll have a confidence interval for your retirement savings that'll likely force some hard decisions. In the next two chapters, I'll show you how to make those hard decisions more comfortable.

HOW TO FIND YOUR TRUE NORTH

"WE MUST NEVER ASSUME THAT
WHICH IS INCAPABLE OF PROOF."

- GEORGE HENRY LEWES, ENGLISH PHILOSOPHER

I'll say it again: Your mathematical model is not as important as your assumptions. The assumptions will make or break the accuracy of your retirement plan.

The common practice is to use historical averages for life expectancies, investment returns, and inflation, but just know those assumptions may have little relationship to your specific circumstances.

The better quality financial planners try to adjust those averages on your behalf. For example, they might change your life expectancy based on family history and personal health.

Some advisors get fancy with Monte Carlo by converting the whole retirement planning process into a probability distribution based on randomized inputs. Others use backcasting calculators to simulate your retirement over actual historical data, basing your future on the past.

There are advantages and disadvantages to each strategy.

In the end, though, the fact of the matter is that *none of these approaches change the results much*. Shocking, but true.

Depending on the confidence interval and assumptions chosen, the Monte Carlo simulation generally allows you to spend between 3 to 5.5 percent. That's remarkably similar to what the ultra-simple dividend discount model produces when using similar assumptions.

All of this is really just common sense once you wrap your head around it. *The amount you can sustainably spend from a portfolio is determined by what it earns after adjusting for inflation, volatility, and sequence of returns.* That's it! You can get as fancy as you want with the math or try to model the impossible, but it won't change this simple truth.

Most everyone reading this book has seen some version of the long-term charts produced by Ibbotson and Associates showing how the long-term returns from large-cap[17] equities approximate 10 percent and inter-mediate-term bonds earn 5 percent. When you factor in inflation assumptions of 3 percent, the net return becomes 7 percent and 2 percent, respectively. This results in a traditional retirement asset allocation mix providing a real return of 3 to 5.5 percent.

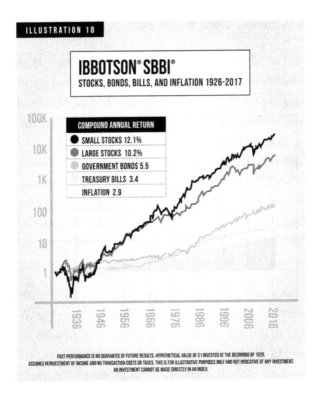

ILLUSTRATION 18

IBBOTSON® SBBI®
STOCKS, BONDS, BILLS, AND INFLATION 1926-2017

COMPOUND ANNUAL RETURN
- SMALL STOCKS 12.1%
- LARGE STOCKS 10.2%
- GOVERNMENT BONDS 5.5
- TREASURY BILLS 3.4
- INFLATION 2.9

PAST PERFORMANCE IS NO GUARANTEE OF FUTURE RESULTS. HYPOTHETICAL VALUE OF $1 INVESTED AT THE BEGINNING OF 1926.
ASSUMES REINVESTMENT OF INCOME AND NO TRANSACTION COSTS OR TAXES. THIS IS FOR ILLUSTRATIVE PURPOSES ONLY AND NOT INDICATIVE OF ANY INVESTMENT.
AN INVESTMENT CANNOT BE MADE DIRECTLY IN AN INDEX.

Is it any wonder that all the retirement calculators are saying you can spend somewhere between 3 percent and 5.5 percent? *It's simple to understand once you see how it's put together.*

To drive that point home, let's examine some retirement planning models that even a math-phobic would love because they're so incredibly simple. You can decide for yourself if their simplicity changes your ideas about how much is enough to retire.

The Beautifully Simple Rule of 25

The first simple model is known as the *Rule of 25*. According to this rule, you figure out how much you'll spend in your first year of retirement (net of pension income, social security, etc. so it's just the shortfall leftover that your portfolio must support) and multiply it by 25 to get the total savings required. This is mathematically the same as saying you can spend 4 percent of your savings—which is right in the middle of our 3 to 5 percent range. But notice how simple the math is—no fancy calculators or computers required. You just multiply your estimated first-year spending by one number.

If you want to get even simpler, then you could rename it the *Rule of 300*, which is nothing more than the *Rule of 25* multiplied by 12 for the number of months in a year (25 x 12 = 300). That way, you can estimate your retirement savings needs in terms of monthly spending because some people prefer to work with monthly numbers. The way the math works is that for every $1,000 you spend monthly from assets (not pensions or social security) in retirement, you'll need roughly $300,000 in a conventional asset allocation portfolio to support that spending for 30 years, adjusted for inflation.

If you're worried about the sequence of returns or choose to retire during a period of high market valuation, there's still no need to get fancy. Instead, you can just make this simple model more conservative by changing it to *The 3 Percent Rule*, also known as the *Rule of 33* for annual spending or the *Rule of 400* for monthly spending. They're all different labels for a more conservative retirement plan that limits first-year spending to 3 percent of assets. This equates to needing 33 times your first-year spending, or roughly 400 times your first month spending if you prefer monthly numbers. Surprisingly, the end result will be close to more elaborate calculator models using similarly conservative assumptions.

HOW TO ADJUST A SIMPLE MODEL TO REDUCE RISK AND MATCH MARKET CONDITIONS

Let's again posit that you need to spend $50,000 from savings during your first year in retirement, so you'll need $1.25 million in total savings (25 x 50,000 = 1,250,000) using the Rule of 25 and $1.65 million for the Rule of 33. Notice how both the required income and assets are very similar to the Dividend Discount Model.

This model is easy to adjust based on market conditions. If interest rates are historically low and/or market valuations are high (or if you want to be conservative) use the 3 percent spending rule built into the *Rule of 33/Rule of 400*. If market valuations are in the bottom 25 percent of the historical range and interest rates are high, then maybe choose a 5 percent spending rule or the *Rule of 20/Rule of 240*.

This flexibility is useful as you decide how conservative you want to be in creating your confidence interval. In my book, *The 4% Rule and Safe Withdrawal Rates in Retirement*, I make a strong case that conclusions based solely on US historical data may be overly optimistic. Wade Pfau tested the 4 percent rule against international historical data in a 2010 *Journal of Financial Planning* article (https://bit.ly/31bn1oz). The result was a stunningly high failure rate for a 4 percent spending rule internationally, and even some risk of failure at 3 percent spending.

With these simple rule-based models, you still get to increase your spending each year by inflation (3 percent in this example) so that you spend $51,500 in your second year, and so on. If you live 30 years in retirement, most of the simulations show the odds of running out of money are very low using domestic data but rise significantly when applied to international data.

Fortunately, there are several simple ways to manage these risks, including:

- You could vary your withdrawals by giving yourself a raise only when your assets grow. Again, you start with the now familiar 4 percent of assets payout as implied by the Rule of 25. Instead of giving yourself an automatic raise based on inflation, you increase spending only when your assets go up, and you maintain a constant payout during years when your portfolio declines. According to simulations, it significantly reduces the risk of outliving your funds.

- You can start with a lower withdrawal percentage—3 percent instead of 4 percent.

- You can set a floor and ceiling on your spending so that it never falls below, or exceeds, a specific percentage of your assets—say, 3 percent on the downside and 6 percent on the upside—regardless of circumstances.

These simple models can work as well as more complex models. Just as important, their simplicity allows you to create a reasonable estimate for your retirement plan sooner than later. They eliminate analysis-paralysis by giving you a "true north" to work toward right now. That way, you can immediately start taking purposeful action to produce tangible results.

ONLY TWO NUMBERS MATTER FOR YOUR RETIREMENT SECURITY

"WHENEVER YOU FIND YOURSELF ON THE SIDE OF THE
MAJORITY, IT IS TIME TO PAUSE AND REFLECT."

- MARK TWAIN, AUTHOR

Some people find it hard to believe these simple methods for calculating your retirement needs are effective because they're so intuitive and easy to work with.

When my Ultimate Retirement Calculator is featured in media coverage about retirement calculators, journalists accustomed to evaluating complex systems note that it doesn't do any of the following:

- *Include separate inputs for each spouse.* (My response: Who needs the complication? Just aggregate both spouses together. It's called community property for a reason.)

- *Provide separate tax rates before and after retirement.* (My response: You're focusing on the wrong issues. Different tax rates would only be marginally meaningful if your income fell dramatically after retirement. Are you planning on poverty or financial security?)

- *Include varying asset allocation with age.* (My response: You can't even model the performance of a single asset allocation accurately for 30 years. The idea that you can model a changing allocation with any greater accuracy is just not realistic.)

The problem is, they're looking for the "magic" number and assume it requires more details and sophisticated modeling to ensure accuracy when no such accuracy is possible.

They don't understand how the math of quality retirement planning works in practice. All those little details are dwarfed in significance by one or two critically important "big numbers" that will make-or-break your analysis. Get these big numbers right, and the rest barely matters. Conversely, get just one of the big numbers wrong and your analysis will fail completely, no matter how many details you got right.

What are those critically important numbers?

#1 Percentage of Income Saved in Your Early Years

In the article on my website, "How Anyone Can Retire in 10 Years (or Less!)," (https://financialmentor.com/10-years) I demonstrate how a super-aggressive savings rate would allow you to skip all the calculators. It involves reducing retirement planning to one simple ratio that forecasts with scientific precision how long it takes to become financially independent. The numbers are as follows:

- 10 percent savings rate = 42 years

- 20 percent savings rate = 32 years

- 40 percent savings rate = 21 years

- 50 percent savings rate = 17 years

- 60 percent savings rate = 14 years

- 70 percent savings rate = 10 years

- 80 percent savings rate = 7 years

(Please note: These numbers are only valid for very high savings rates of 60 to 80 percent because longer time horizons introduce complications from compounding investment returns and inflation. Lower savings rates or longer time horizons are shown for illustration only. See the full article for all the details: https://financialmentor.com/10-years.*)*

This is not some crazy math theory. It explains exactly how I retired at age 35. I saved roughly 70 percent of a substantial income and never allowed spending to rise with income. It didn't take long for my assets to grow sufficiently large to support my lifestyle.

It's a simple and foolproof way to retire young and know

with certainty how much money you need. No fancy math, impossible assumptions, or retirement calculators required. It just plain works as long as you can make enough to save that high percentage of your income and still live a comfortable life.

The key principle to takeaway is if you want to retire faster, reduce your spending, or raise your income so your savings as a percent of income grows. The higher the percentage savings, the faster and more reliably you'll reach your financial independence goal.

In a National Bureau of Economic Research report (https://bit.ly/2Kte6cc), economists analyzed accumulated wealth in families from all walks of life and income levels to determine why some high-income families end up with little wealth while other low-income families accumulate significant wealth.

Surprisingly, their results show no statistical difference for ending wealth due to income, investment strategies, or life circumstances. As it turned out, **the number one determinant of lifetime wealth is an individual's savings rate**. (I'll add that savings rate is primarily important in the early years of wealth accumulation and is replaced by the second critical number, as explained below, once significant assets have been accumulated.)

Again, don't get hung up on distracting details. Just pay attention to your savings rate in relation to your earnings. It's the first of two critically important numbers.

#2 RETURN ON INVESTMENT MINUS INFLATION

Your investment return minus inflation comes second only because of when it occurs in time, not due to its relative importance.

The investment return assumption is the critical number (along with inflation) determining your retirement failure or success. The first half of your financial life is dominated by your savings rate and the accumulation of assets. But the investment return assumption dominates your retirement security in the second half of your financial life once you accumulate significant assets.

The relationship between inflation and portfolio return will literally make or break your retirement. It is *The Big One*. Nothing else comes close when planning retirement with paper assets, which is why we spent several chapters exploring this assumption earlier.

The reason it's so important is simple: Compound returns multiply little differences into huge differences over long periods. This isn't about turning molehills into mountains; this is about turning grains of sand into the Himalayas.

I'll repeat that point for emphasis because I don't want you to miss it. *Both inflation and return on investment have a compounded effect on your estimate for how much money you need to retire.* That's why they're both critically important, and why the amount of money you need to retire is determined mainly by the net difference between those two numbers. The only other number that even comes close in importance is your savings rate as a percent of your income, as previously discussed.

Don't take my word for it. Prove it to yourself right now. Go to my Ultimate Retirement Calculator (https://financial mentor.com/retirement-calculator) and enter the numbers that best represent your life situation. Seriously, do it before reading on. It'll only take two minutes. Don't worry about perfection. Your best estimates from the earlier exercise are good enough for this one.

When inputting your expected lifespan, use age 100 unless you have known health issues. Notice how the calculator allows you to reduce spending during retirement. Once you fill out the calculator with your base level numbers, press the "calculate" button to get your total then write down the "magic retirement number" so you can refer back to it.

Next, try perfecting your magic number by tweaking a few variables like tax rate, retirement age, and other details. Don't change either of the two key inputs highlighted in this chapter—return on investment and inflation, or savings rate as a percent of income. Everything else is fair game.

Notice that your magic number changes with each variation, but the changes are marginal. Your estimates for how much money you need to retire remain in the same ballpark as your original number. The calculation is relatively stable.

Now, using the exact same inputs as before, raise your inflation rate by 2 percent while simultaneously reducing your return on investment by 2 percent, but make sure you're sitting down first.

See what I mean? For most people, this small change will literally multiply the amount you need to retire several fold. It should knock your original estimate right out of the ballpark, over the river, and into the next state.

That is why I call all the other variables "details" and label these two ratios "critical." It's just the way the math works.

> **Principle:** Small changes in a few key numbers multiplied over long periods have huge impacts on your ability to retire with financial security. Therefore, focus on those key variables and don't worry about the multitude of details.

THE SMART WAY TO USE
RETIREMENT CALCULATORS

"TODAY'S SCIENTISTS HAVE SUBSTITUTED MATHEMATICS FOR EXPERIMENTS, AND THEY WANDER OFF THROUGH EQUATION AFTER EQUATION, AND EVENTUALLY BUILD A STRUCTURE WHICH HAS NO RELATION TO REALITY."

- NIKOLA TESLA, INVENTOR

You've now witnessed the instability of retirement modeling. Changing a few key numbers makes the entire prediction inaccurate, so is there any value in modeling your retirement at all? After all, what's the point in calculating how much money you need to retire if it could be two times or four times larger than your estimate?

There is still a lot of value in using a retirement calculator, but not for the reasons that are traditionally taught. Instead, I find it helpful for putting numbers to life scenarios and investment strategies and seeing how changing my plans changes the numbers.

MODEL LIFE SCENARIOS — NOT MAGIC NUMBERS

I call this *scenario analysis*, and here are some different ways to apply it in your retirement planning:

- Use retirement calculators to model a wide range of variables to produce a confidence interval estimating the assets you supposedly need.

- See what happens if you add 10 years of additional income—part-time work, consulting, or whatever might interest you—to take the pressure off savings and allow your assets more time to grow.

- Test the strategy of replacing part of your paper asset portfolio with real estate rental income that adjusts for inflation and rises when you pay off the mortgage.

- Simulate the impact of receiving a lump sum inheritance, selling a home, or maybe a business.

- Try replacing a portion of your portfolio with the purchase of a longevity annuity that starts paying at age 80 until death. Notice how you can safely increase your asset depletion in the early years when playing with this strategy.

- Model the difference between a conventional asset allocation and a dividend growth[18] portfolio. Should you increase the bond allocation as conventional financial planning advocates, or should you concentrate in other assets?

- Find out how the numbers change when you delay social security but the eventual monthly check is larger, or you start payments early but receive less each month.

- Now that you've tested a bunch of different ideas, try mixing and matching several factors together, and notice what happens.

In other words, use the retirement calculator to put numbers behind different life plans for your financial future. Each scenario will teach you a valuable retirement planning principle. *Retirement planning done right is really about life planning*, not calculating magic numbers.

My Ultimate Retirement Calculator is designed specifically to provide a simple process for scenario analysis. It allows you to easily model different scenarios that fit both your desired lifestyle and financial situation.

The Ultimate Retirement Calculator is designed with three specific objectives in mind:

1. It omits meaningless complication and nonessential details, reducing obstacles to completing the calculations. It's better to plan retirement roughly than not do it at all. It's also important to not get so caught up in minute

details that you deceive yourself into believing the output is scientifically accurate. Remember, it's just a few key numbers that will make or break your plans.

2. It provides a simplified platform so you can model various real-life scenarios using all three asset classes (not just paper assets). No other calculator allows that flexibility, which is essential for the way modern retirements are planned.

3. It allows you to quickly and easily build confidence intervals by varying single inputs and seeing how it affects overall output.

In short, this calculator is designed for scenario analysis—not "magic" numbers—because that's what is useful when estimating how much money you need to retire. The common mistake is to make the process exclusively about asset accumulation when there's far greater value in the life planning aspect.

Calculators are best used for mapping a path and putting numbers behind your life plan. They're indispensable for seeing the financial impact of "What if...?" scenarios so you can make better-informed decisions about your future.

Scenario analysis is how you blend life planning with retirement calculators to engineer a realistic roadmap for achieving financial security. It's a practical approach for retirement planning that avoids the myths and traps that, unfortunately, have become conventional wisdom. It acknowledges the inherent limitations in designing an asset-based retirement plan and provides a practical solution.

WALK YOUR CALCULATION FORWARD — DON'T SET IT AND FORGET IT

The other way to increase your retirement security using the traditional model (after scenario analysis) is to walk your estimate forward in time by replacing estimated assumptions with actual data as the years roll by. It's another smart way to use retirement calculators.

This strategy was mentioned earlier, but it's worth repeating here now that you understand the critical role of the two key numbers in your retirement plan and the possibility that small errors can compound into big problems.

The walk forward process cuts that problem off at the knees by replacing assumptions with actual results. Each iteration of your retirement plan progressively fixes each assumption error, so the total error gets reduced to a manageable size.

It works like a guided missile flying to a target across vast distances. The missile will spend more time during its flight off-target than on-target because of wind and other factors, but the guidance system will constantly course-correct, making small changes until it finally hits the target with precision. Walk forward modeling is the "guidance system" that keeps your retirement plan on target.

This is another reason the traditional model is useful, despite its inherent shortcomings. Because it's based on assets, you can use it as an accountability process to track the progress of your retirement in flight and course-correct throughout the journey. You just keep fixing all the small assumption errors that inevitably occur during retirement so none of them can compound into a catastrophic failure. The result is financial security and a very low risk of failure using the traditional model, in spite of the instability of its assumptions. *In other words, this is how you create security out of uncertainty.*

In summary, below are five rules to help you get value out of the traditional retirement planning model and use retirement calculators the smart way.

1. **Walk Forward Process:** Don't perform the retirement savings goal exercise once, put it on a shelf, and then forget it. Instead, check back every few years, and see what assumptions proved valid and which ones did not. Adjust your assumptions, recalculate, and shift your plans accordingly. Rinse and repeat every few years. This way you'll hit your retirement goal like a rocket continuously course-correcting toward its target.

2. **Errors Multiply:** Small errors in estimates compound into large errors in results. Retirement savings are built and spent over multiple decades. A 2 percent error in inflation or investment return that is manageable over 5 to 10 years is a complete disaster when compounded over 30 to 40 years. That's why you must regularly recalibrate over time, based on actual results. Small details in key numbers cause huge differences, so pay particularly close attention to the key numbers.

3. **Teach Principles:** The traditional model using a retirement calculator is valuable for teaching essential retirement planning principles. After just a few quick scenario tests, users quickly grasp how investment return net of inflation is the most important number. You also see the importance of time in compounding your way to wealth versus saving your way to wealth without the benefit of compound returns over time. You see the erosive effect of inflation by watching how your spending escalates out of control. Without a calculator, these concepts are difficult to grasp, but with a calculator, they become obvious.

4. **Scenario Analysis:** Use the calculator to quantify different life plans. Try substituting cash flow assets for growth assets, extend retirement dates, or replace part-time income that might be enjoyed for decades into the future for full-time income now that might lead to burnout and early retire-

ment. The point is to put hard numbers behind "squishy" life plans that may be hard to quantify so you can see the results.

5. **Maintain Flexibility**: Avoid calculators that limit your ability to change assumptions. It's shocking how many calculators preprogram assumptions for investment return, inflation, longevity, and other essential inputs. When an assumption is hard-coded into a calculator, it reduces your ability to plan scenarios.

In other words, use retirement calculators with an asset-based, traditional retirement plan to test, hypothesize, and track your retirement future. They're handy when properly applied and understood.

It may seem like the task is impossible, given the magnitude of potential error. But with enough practice in scenario analysis and walk forward planning, you'll find acceptable workarounds and solutions so you can plan your life in a way that will result in long-term financial security.

This brings you to an important turn in your retirement planning education because it completes Model 1 by showing you how to use the traditional asset-based model the smart way. In the remainder of this book, you'll build on top of that first model by applying two additional retirement planning frameworks to create a robust retirement that perfectly fits your personal situation and plans for the future.

In other words, what I'll show you is the complete answer to how much money you need to retire is a three-step process where the traditional model (what you've learned about so far) is the essential first step. Now it's time to build on that foundational knowledge with two additional steps to form a complete picture.

1. The first step is scenario analysis built on the traditional model framework. That's what you've learned about so far.

2. The second step (as explained in the next chapter) is creative lifestyle planning that takes maximum advantage of the critical numbers that make or break your retirement.

3. The third step (explained in the final chapter) is the cash flow-based model that provides the last piece of your puzzle by showing you the most secure, but difficult to achieve, retirement plan.

4. Also, I provide a "Retirement Calculator Secrets" video course (https://financialmentor.com/calculator-course) showing you how to strategically implement all of these strategies using the free Ultimate Retirement Calculator (https://financialmentor.com/retirement-calculator).

Each of these three retirement planning tools stands on the foundation of the traditional model, with all its shortcomings. You learned its limitations and its value, allowing you to implement the three creative solutions that will lead to your financial security in retirement.

Now let's turn to the next chapter where you'll apply the first creative solution using scenario analysis to shave years off your retirement date, reduce risk, and increase financial security—all at the same time.

MODEL 2

LIFESTYLE PLANNING, THE CREATIVE WAY

FLIP THE SCRIPT ON YOUR RETIREMENT

"OUR LIFE IS FRITTERED AWAY BY DETAIL. SIMPLIFY, SIMPLIFY."

- HENRY DAVID THOREAU, WRITER AND PHILOSOPHER

The standard advice for retirement planning is that you should save as much as you can, starting as early as you can, to maximize your savings at each point in time. The more you can allocate to your retirement account, the longer it will compound, and the easier it will be to achieve your retirement goals.

Nothing new there. You've heard it 100 times before.

However, think back to a time when you had far less money than today, but you were happier. Maybe that time was college. You were broke, and life was still good. You were learning and growing, had great friends, and lots of fun. Money wasn't plentiful, but you got creative and figured out how to make things work. You found the best happy hour spots with the best deals. You didn't buy furniture to look rich because it was all about function, not form. Notice the disconnect between your spending, lifestyle, and how fulfilling and fun life can be?

One of the happiest times in my life was living with three buddies in a one-bedroom apartment during my senior year in college. We didn't even have our own beds; there wasn't enough room, so you just slept where you could. All of my worldly possessions fit in a coat closet in the entryway, and the fridge was always empty. But I was learning a ton from my classes, and we were (and are) great friends. The reason it worked is because we had the important stuff right—the details didn't matter.

Would it be so bad to live like that, even if you're making six figures? A lot of the fun of college life came from the creativity you had to apply to afford what you really wanted. The remainder came from living in a way that emphasized personal growth and close relationships.

The point is, there are many ways to make your life more fulfilling that have no connection to spending money. This may fly in the face of conventional consumer-driven values, but it works. Not only that, it's easy and fun.

Traditional retirement planning, however, operates from an implied assumption: You're supposed to pile up a big nest egg to pay for your future lifestyle. But imagine turning that equation upside-down by questioning your assumptions about lifestyle so you need less nest egg? What would happen if you envisioned your life plan first, from the ground up? Maybe, just maybe, you might find that life would become a lot more fulfilling and a lot smaller nest egg would be required to pay for it.

I'm not talking about eating beans and rice for the rest of your life or shopping in thrift stores. Instead, this is about questioning what makes you happy. Surprisingly, many people find happiness doesn't cost much money. Even more shocking is how much of the stuff you're sacrificing your life to pay for right now may not be all that fulfilling.

When you reset your life plan first, it turns traditional retirement planning upside-down. This strategy is smart because the whole point of financial freedom is to lead a more fulfilling life. And the good news is that prioritizing what matters most to you usually costs a LOT LESS than you ever imagined.

The Chicken or the Egg — Assets or Spending?

The simple, yet inviolable, rule supporting this strategy is that the amount of assets required to buy your financial freedom is a multiple of your spending.

Sure, there are a lot of mathematical models designed to calculate your retirement number. And yes, they each give slightly varied results, but it's not significant.

For the standard set of assumptions, the range of expected withdrawal rates from savings varies between 3 percent and 5.5 percent. Whether you use simple models, sophisticated Monte Carlo analysis, conventional models, or valuation-based models, you should expect a result somewhere in that narrowly defined range. For purposes of this discussion on creative strategies, we'll use 4 percent to keep things simple (please see my companion book *The 4% Rule and Safe Withdrawal Rates in Retirement* for a complete analysis).

That means standard approaches to retirement planning are somewhat confined without much room for creativity. If your financial situation doesn't fit the conventional mold, then you're stuck. However, you've learned in these pages that the whole retirement planning process breaks down to the question of figuring out how to get your annual expenses under 4 percent of your invested savings. Or, stated more simply, your financial independence is a formula where the assets required are a multiple of your spending. That perspective opens the door to creative solutions that bend traditional rules.

- If you spend less, then you need fewer assets.

- If you spend less, then you save more assets more quickly.

- If your assets earn more, then you need fewer assets to support the same level of spending.

This simple understanding of spending relative to the assets required to support spending explains why a person who needs $20,000 per year is rich when she has a million dollars, but a person who spends $150,000 per year feels poor with a million dollars. It's the same portfolio but a totally different life experience.

Where retirement planning gets exciting is when you start playing with these key relationships (expenses vs. assets, cash flow vs. asset amortization, and/or investment return vs. inflation) to find creative retirement planning solutions. It turns the boring, confined world of conventional retirement planning into a creative exercise in life planning.

For example, the obvious ways to make the biggest impact are:

- Reducing your expenses (increases savings rate and reduces total savings needed).

- Adding preretirement sources of income (increases savings rate).

- Optimizing how you manage money (really just a twist on reducing expenses above, but it leads to different strategies).

- Adding post-retirement income (reduces or eliminates any need for savings).

- Improving investment returns (reduces needed savings).

If you want to close a savings gap or retire a lot sooner, you'll want to combine these strategies. Keep in mind that you get big variations in the amount of savings required to retire by *changing the assumptions you put into the model, not the model itself.* The more assumptions you change, the bigger the difference in the savings you need.

A secret to strategic retirement planning is to focus

your creativity on the thing that matters the most: Your assumptions. This is where the game gets fun. Readers frequently tell me this is the most empowering, life-changing part of this entire book.

Scenario Analysis Revisited

Right now, your retirement is built around a single, hypothetical life scenario. But you aren't stuck with just one life plan and one set of assumptions. You can imagine many different ways you might like to live, and then you can see how those new assumptions change the amount of money you need to retire.

I've worked with coaching clients to apply my ideas and watched them go speechless when they realized a lifetime of financial independence was already within their grasp—right now—by making just a few life changes. These weren't isolated cases; it happened frequently. These clients realized how making a few life changes was a small price to pay for a lifetime of freedom, and it could happen to you too.

At a minimum, you should be able to cut a decade or more off your financial plan. These are literally life-changing ideas when you get creative and figure out what the life that will make you happy really costs. You just might be positively surprised.

How It Works

In this chapter, I'll introduce a long list of alternative scenarios for you to try on for size, like a set of clothes. Some of these ideas will fit, and others will look hideous on you. That's okay, discard what you don't like, and keep what works for you.

Your goal is to think long and hard about how you can apply each idea to your life. Brainstorm with your partner or a friend over a glass of wine. Be wacky, and offer up crazy ideas because you don't know where it might take your thinking. The more creative you get, the more dramatic the results you'll produce with this process.

Next, take your favorite ideas to my Ultimate Retirement Calculator for advanced scenario planning, and apply them against the benchmark model you created using your standard assumptions in the earlier chapter. You'll test each idea, one by one, to see the impact. Watch how your numbers change before your eyes. It's serious fun.

I'll show you how this process works with three examples before giving you the entire brainstorming list. Those examples will define the rules and parameters of the creative retirement planning game. Once the boundaries are defined, you'll get a whole series of brainstorming suggestions to solve various assumption problems and manage specific risks. Your only responsibility is to pick and choose what fits your needs from the list so that you can assemble your own creative solutions.

Example 1: Cut the Big Expenses First

Let's start with the first assumption: The amount of money you need to spend in retirement. The Rule of 25 (Rule of 300, if monthly) tells you that for every $12,000 you can shave off your annual retirement budget ($1,000 per month), you'll reduce your savings required by roughly $300,000. That's a big deal.

Most people find it a lot easier to live happily-ever-after on just $1,000 per month less than to figure out how to save another $300,000. Below are some different lifestyle choices for you to consider that will put this idea to work in your plan:

- You could relocate to a smaller house in the same area.

- You could relocate to a lower-cost area, including those states without income tax such as Nevada, Washington, or Texas.

- You could travel full-time in an RV enjoying the outdoor recreation lifestyle.

- You could move to a lower-cost foreign country like Mexico or Ecuador, or maybe consider a country like Canada with better healthcare benefits.

The list of ways to save money is endless. However, *the smart strategy is to start with the biggest expenses*—housing, taxes, and healthcare— and work your way down from there. The large budget items are how you get the most significant financial improvement for each life change. Spending less doesn't have to mean less happiness, but it absolutely will mean a lot less retirement savings burden.

For example, I recently met a 72-year-old campground host who was having the best time of his life spending eight months out of the year in the deep forests of Paradise, Oregon. He spent the remaining four months with his family on the beaches of Mexico. He was putting money in his pocket and living with joy in some of the most beautiful places in the world.

Another example is Billy and Akaisha Kaderli (https:// bit.ly/2Kw9XnU), who both retired from brokerage and restaurant businesses at age 38 in 1991 and began to travel the world. Today, they augment their income with an online business sharing their early retirement story. The end result is financial freedom when many people are still trying to figure out how to pay their bills.

Your creativity is the only limit to how far you can take this strategy. I've seen many coaching clients who reformulate their retirement for greater happiness while reducing their savings requirement by over $1,000,000. Surprisingly, it's not that hard. They just get creative on what best aligns with their values to make them happy.

If you really want to get extreme, then maybe you can figure out how to live in retirement bliss on just $25,000 per year. That would allow you to live off social security or a small pension and never save a dime. This may sound far-fetched, but use it as a challenge to reformulate what you really need to be happy. Retirement gives you a chance to start all over again, so toss your old spending rules out the door and question every assumption.

EXAMPLE 2: POST-RETIREMENT INCOME

This second example adds a twist to how standard retirement planning works with social security and pensions. It's best to reframe this category into "residual income" because that reframe opens your mind to many other possibilities that might be overlooked.

Consider:

- Income-producing real estate can provide an income stream you never outlive, with the added advantage that it grows over time to offset inflation.

- Income from a lifestyle business or hobby business reduces retirement savings needs just like reduced spending. It's mathematically the same thing. For every $1,000 per month earned during retirement, you reduce savings needs by roughly $300,000.

- Dividend-paying stocks can provide an income stream you can never outlive because they historically have grown faster than inflation to preserve purchasing power.

- Fixed annuities[19] can provide income for life and often pay a higher yield than comparable fixed income securities like bonds. This allows you to shift the longevity risk to the insurance company.

- Speaking of longevity risk, you could buy a longevity annuity that will pay only after age 80 (assuming you live that long). That allows you to safely spend more by amortizing your savings more aggressively since they only have to last until the longevity annuity starts.

For example, we assumed in our earlier hypothetical example a spending requirement of $100,000 with $50,000 coming from social security and pensions, leaving $50,000 to be made up from savings. Per the Rule of 300, for every additional $1,000 of monthly residual income you produce, you lower your savings requirement by roughly $300,000. Let's say you fixed up an old house and rented it out to provide an extra $1,000 per month above mortgage and expenses. You've just reduced your savings requirement by $300,000 and added a source of income that should grow with inflation.

Now, let's put the first two steps together and see the combined impact. Let's say you downsize your home to a lower-cost location and travel six months out of the year in your RV. These two changes might lower your spending from $100,000 per year to $75,000 per year. Let's also assume you prepared for your retirement by purchasing a four-plex apartment building while in your fifties that is now fully paid off and produces an extra $2,000 per month.

Assuming you still get the $50,000 from social security and a small pension, *your savings requirements are now basically zero.* Sure, you'll want to maintain a little rainy day nest egg, but you won't need the $1,000,000+ nest egg previously required. That's a radical difference for making two minor adjustments.

Example 3: Alternative Investment Strategy

If that's not enough to get you excited, then this third strategy will challenge yet another assumption—your investment return minus inflation. Traditional retirement planning assumes you have a passive, buy-and-hold portfolio with a conventional asset allocation that produces typical returns. Let's assume 8 percent annual returns as a reasonable, long-term number. When you net out inflation (assume 3 percent for simplicity), that leaves 5 percent or a 0.05 net return. Using the Dividend Discount Model and our previous example, you needed $1,000,000 in savings to throw off $50,000 in retirement income ($50,000/0.05).

Now, suppose your investment skill produced 18 percent returns instead of 8 percent. The effect on the savings required is dramatic. Assuming 3 percent inflation gives a net return of 15 percent or 0.15. Using the same Dividend Discount Model and dividing $50,000 by 0.15 results in $333,333 required savings. *Notice how roughly doubling the return on your investments cut the savings required by two-thirds.* That is dramatic.

I know most investors don't have the skill to produce outsized investment returns with consistency in the financial markets. But it's not a stretch for people to generate outsized returns in nontraditional retirement assets such as real estate and business. Again, you're limited only by your imagination, skill, and determination. I'm just trying to show the possibilities:

- You can acquire a rental property (or two) in your forties or fifties so you have inflation-adjusting income for the rest of your life.

- You can learn investment skills now so you aren't bound by passive investment return assumptions when you retire.

- You could start a side hustle, part-time business that you enjoy so much you'd never want to retire from it.

- You could build a business during your working career then sell it for a large payday.

- You could build a business that you designed

from the beginning as a semi-passive cash flow strategy.

- You could convert a portion of your conventional portfolio into positive cash flow real estate sufficient to pay your bills.

- You could convert your existing home into multiple rental units.

- You could launch an Airbnb business out of your home using extra space, including children's rooms after they move out.

- Or you could convert your garage into a rental unit.

Some of these investment ideas may sound difficult to accomplish, others easy. Regardless, you'll find it's empowering and also easier to close a retirement savings gap through lifestyle changes than by figuring out how to stash away an extra few million dollars between now and retirement day.

COMPLETE BRAINSTORMING LIST FOR THE LIFESTYLE MODEL

Now that you have a clear idea how this works, here is a comprehensive list of strategies, including earlier ideas, to consider when applying creativity to your retirement plan.

Buckets of Risk: Rather than treat your retirement

income and assets as one big bucket, consider breaking it into two buckets: "Must have" and "nice to have." The way this works in practice is to decide what income is necessary for all your basic needs—food, water, shelter, health insurance, etc. Then supplement your fixed income from pensions and social security payments with enough inflation adjusting fixed annuities to pay for all your basic needs, eliminating the risk that you will outlive your money.

This method has several advantages:

- Fixed annuities may pay a higher return than your safe withdrawal rate. Insurance companies can afford to do this because they keep all the money not paid out to the people who die early.

- You transfer the risk of outliving your assets or suffering through outsized investment losses to the insurance company and government.

- Your "basic needs" number is smaller than the "all expenses included" number, making retirement savings less daunting.

- You can afford to play the probability games a bit tighter and be a bit more aggressive on your spending with remaining assets because if that portion of your savings only lasts to age 85, it's not a catastrophe. Your basic needs are still covered, and you enjoyed spending the money while your health was still vibrant.

I really like this strategy—a lot. You may want to seriously consider it. It's a simple but elegant solution to more problems in retirement planning than space allows me to explain. The more you play with this solution, the more you'll find to like about it.

If you choose this approach and purchase annuities, it's imperative that you check the financial strength of the insurance company before committing your hard-earned dollars. An insurance contract is only as strong as the company that stands behind it.

Additionally, just in case something goes wrong, you should know the limit for guarantee association coverage in your state. Consider diversifying your annuity purchases to stay within coverage limits by only buying limited amounts from each provider. In other words, if your state's guarantee association limits coverage to $100,000, then don't buy more than $100,000 of coverage from any one provider.

I explain many more essential principles about annuities in my book, *Variable Annuity Pros and Cons.* You can get the scoop on my pro-consumer advocate position analyzing other life insurance investment products at https://financialmentor.com/life-insurance.

Longevity Annuity: Another creative solution using life insurance annuity products is to consider a longevity annuity.

For example, some longevity annuities begin payment at

age 80 and continue paying for the remainder of your life. If you purchase enough coverage to pay all your required bills, you can spend much more aggressively from savings because you have a shorter, defined amortization period for your assets. You can afford to run out of money at age 80 because your longevity annuity will pick up the difference.

The advantage of this product is you don't have to "self-insure" an unknowable life expectancy because your longevity annuity takes care of that risk. Better yet, that coverage is often more affordable than self-insuring by assuming a long lifespan. The reason it's reasonably affordable is that insurance companies base pricing on the actuarial risk of expected lifespan. They know a certain percentage of their customers will never collect on the policy, and most that do collect cost them very little based on the average remaining lifespan. You don't have that same luxury since you are a sample size of one, making longevity annuities a potentially cost-efficient solution.

Extreme Frugality: Most people increase their expenses and lifestyle as their income rises. I chose not to do that by living a college student lifestyle on a very high income as a hedge fund[20] manager. This one decision allowed me to save 70 percent of everything earned and retire comfortably at age 35. This approach is not for everyone, but it's proven effective. It was easy for me because my income was large, and my needs were small as a single male who loves books and outdoor recreation. Other people achieve the same result on much lower incomes than mine by living in an RV, using public transportation or riding a bike, shopping in thrift stores, and growing their own food.

Stated another way, some people prefer to work at saving money rather than work at earning it. It's not for everyone, but I'd be remiss not to list it because it's a very effective strategy. Not only does extreme frugality dramatically increase your savings rate as a percent of income (which, as stated earlier, is one of the two most important numbers in retirement planning), but it can also dramatically reduce how much money you need to retire. It can make you financially independent in just a few years—albeit at a low spending level.

Time: Focus on the right strategies for the time remaining to achieve your goals.

For example, personal finance authors love to extoll the virtues of compound returns as the Eighth Wonder of the World, but the truth is that compound returns are irrelevant when time is short. If you don't have a lot of years to achieve your financial goals, your primary equation is built around spending and asset accumulation, with less importance on investment return.

When your time to retirement is short, you need to strategize from both ends—saving and spending—because investment considerations won't make a material difference. It takes many years for a 2 percent increase in investment return to demonstrate its value.

Conversely, if your time horizon is long (i.e., a 20-year-old planning to retire at 60 and live to 100), then investment return net of inflation will dwarf all other numbers combined. Additionally, when you're young, it's more valuable to get an early start on aggressive saving because those first dollars have many, many years to compound. Every dollar bill you spend in your twenties is like spending a hundred dollar bill in retirement.

The point is that you want to match your creative strategies to your time horizon. When time is short, focus on spending strategies and asset accumulation, and when time is long, focus on investment return net of inflation with early savings. This is a key principle.

Convert Hobbies into Income: Maybe you love to fly airplanes, build wire sculptures, sew, or in my case, write about finance. You can convert that passion into income. Even if it only pays $2,000 per month, that can take tremendous pressure off your savings, give you a sense of purpose, and connect you to a community. When it is work that you love, then it's not work at all. Plus, that extra $2,000 reduces your retirement savings needs by $600,000 to $800,000, which isn't bad considering it's something you love to do anyway.

Phased Work: The biggest problem with most jobs is that they leave no time to live your life. Rather than quit cold-turkey, consider a part-time or phased career so you have some income along with time to pursue your dreams. For example, an accountant could prepare tax returns during the busiest four months of the year and take the other eight months to travel the world. A real estate professional could work as a team member to a top-performing sales leader during the busy summer season and spend the winter skiing. A doctor could fill in for some on-call shifts when not traveling or during the summer vacation season when the staff wants time off.

Phased work is a powerful strategy because it reduces the total number of years your assets must support you in retirement, plus it extends the time that your assets can grow. This one-two combination both reduces how much money you need to retire and grows your nest egg at the same time.

Repurpose Your Real Estate Equity to Income: If the kids moved out and you find yourself with more home than you really need, there are a variety of strategies that can put that extra equity to work for you.

- Maybe you could build a "mother-in-law" quarters.

- You could convert an unused basement or attic into a rental unit that produces perpetual income in your retirement.

- Extra bedrooms could be repurposed into Airbnb units.

- Or maybe you sell that big house and convert the equity into a duplex or four-plex so you have rental income you can never outlive while still having the privacy of your own apartment.

What's great about this strategy is you don't have to tie up more of your assets in real estate, but your passive income increases. You get more cash flow for the same amount of equity.

Inflation Risks: If you're concerned about inflation, then consider investment strategies specifically designed to manage that risk. For example, on the fixed income side, you may want to choose TIPS[21] over regular bonds. On the equity side, you may want to look at dividend growth stocks over traditional equity allocations[22] to capture the fact that both dividend payments and stock growth rates historically have outpaced inflation.

However, if you pursue this strategy, be careful to always focus your strategy on total return on investment so that you don't become falsely enamored with income only. In other words, there's a danger with income investing that pursuing cash flow can cause your total return to drop, which would be a negative to your retirement plan (despite the income). Total return is what actually matters.

Another investment strategy to help manage inflation risk is purchasing rental real estate with the expectation that your rental rates will grow with inflation, along with the value of the property. The advantage of this investment strategy is it simplifies the math of your retirement plan by eliminating inflation growth both from the expense and the investment side of the equation. Just be careful to reduce your investment return assumptions accordingly if you decide to pursue this approach because much of the historical capital growth in real estate is really just inflation.

Retire Based on Market Valuations: Match the amount you can spend from your retirement nest egg to what research says can be supported, given market valuations and interest rates on the date you retire.

In other words, rather than choose your spending based on your income needs, choose your spending based on what research says your assets and market conditions can support. If the markets are in the top quartile of historical valuations when you retire, then start with very conservative spending plans. Alternatively, it might make sense to consider inflation-adjusting fixed annuities instead of a traditional 60/40 asset allocation mix.

However, if you're lucky and the investment markets are in the bottom quartile of historical valuations when you retire, then maybe you can afford to plan for more aggressive spending from savings or increase your stock allocation.

And if the numbers don't work because expected returns are unreasonably low given overvalued markets, then another possibility is to choose your retirement date so it coincides with a market valuation that gives you a higher expected return and a lower sequence of returns risk during those critical first 10 to 15 years of your retirement.

Longevity Risk Management Strategies: If you're worried about outliving your assets, here are three great strategies to consider:

- The first is to annuitize[23] enough of your assets to cover at least your necessary living expenses using the previously mentioned "buckets of risk" strategy. This shifts the risk of living a very long life to your insurance company.

- Alternatively, you could purchase longevity insurance annuities[24] that only start paying at an advanced age, such as age 80. They are quite affordable and will allow you to budget a higher level of spending from your other assets knowing the annuity will kick in if you live longer.

- Finally, the third strategy is to budget your spending to last until age 85 while living in your fully-paid-for home. If your money runs out before you die, then you can just sell your home or do a reverse mortgage to harvest the equity and pay for any additional years.

Better yet, you could combine these three strategies any way you want. For example, selling your free-and-clear home at age 80 will give a big boost to assets at a time where you won't be spending much because you're older, your longevity insurance contract just started paying, and your other annuity contract continues to pay. This combination strategy can give you excellent security in your older years.

The goal for all of these strategies is to manage your longevity risk so you can afford to spend more aggressively from principal because the time your assets must survive is narrowly defined.

Choose an Unconventional Spending Pattern: Much of the research into safe withdrawal rates from your retirement savings assumes you increase spending each year at the rate of inflation. I already showed you that assumption is likely aggressive, resulting in higher spending in your later years than is necessary.

One idea is to consider choosing a different spending pattern that involves spending more in your early years of retirement, but then you don't adjust that spending upward for inflation later on. You just commit to managing your spending so it doesn't escalate, or possibly declines. Potential spending patterns include:

- Only allow spending increases for inflation during years when your portfolio increases in value.

- Fix your spending as a percent of your portfolio, regardless of the portfolio value, so you only get increases when the portfolio goes up and suffer through decreases in spending when the portfolio goes down.

- Place guardrails on your spending (like 3 percent of assets as a minimum and 6 percent as a maximum) so it can never exceed an upper threshold or decline below a bottom threshold. This reduces the risk of spending too much and running out of money before you run out of life or spending too little principal and forsaking a lifestyle you might have enjoyed.

By varying your spending so that you don't automatically increase annually with inflation, you'll find there are a variety of options that will allow a higher percentage of the expense in the early years while reducing your risk of failure.

PICK THE PRICE YOU'LL PAY

Each creative life planning choice gives you another way to take back control and plan a secure financial future. Your retirement plan must fit your life vision, and you're empowered to create it in any way that works for you. It is not bound by the confines of the conventional model.

However, you also need to know there's a price to pay, no matter which path you choose. Every creative choice requires lifestyle tradeoffs, and only you can decide what tradeoffs best reflect your values.

To illustrate the point, consider three different retirement plan scenarios: Aggressive early, moderate middle, and relaxed old. All three of these scenarios are mathematically possible using a conventional asset model, but each reflects very different trade-offs.

- **Aggressive Early**: You could retire in your thirties, or maybe early forties, by saving aggressively and living frugally throughout your career (or creating a business or real estate portfolio using the advanced planning framework as taught in this course https://financialmentor.com/3). If you place a higher priority on the freedom of not having a job than you do on enjoying some luxuries in life, and you find satisfaction by living on less, then this might work well for you. The price you pay is the constant need to optimize your spending choices based on the right side of the menu of life. What you gain is the freedom to do what you want much earlier in life, but all those decisions must be made within the confines of your self-imposed spending limitations.

- **Moderate Middle**: Alternatively, you could work another decade or two retiring in your late forties or fifties by saving prudently but still living moderately. You'll still need to budget, save where you can, repair instead of replace, and choose Toyotas over Ferraris and jeans over designer duds. But you can live comfortably with careful planning and gain a decade of freedom in the process.

- **Relaxed Old:** This longer timeframe gives you decades more to compound your wealth so your monthly savings requirements are lower and your assets have longer to grow. You end up with a larger retirement nest egg (albeit, later in life) and fewer years that the nest egg has to support your spending. That means you can spend more during your earning years and spend more in retirement. The price you pay is working for decades longer, which is fine if you love your work and find it fulfilling, but not so smart if you don't.

The point is each of these paths represents trade-offs. I've seen smart people choose any of the timeframes listed above and make them work, building a uniquely personal plan to fit their values. There is no single right answer. Instead, it's about looking at all the lifestyle choices and various planning alternatives and figuring out what works for you.

It would be sad to live frugally, saving millions, then get hit by a bus at age 40 never having enjoyed any of the money. Conversely, it would be equally sad to enjoy every last dime as it is earned, living permanently on the financial edge, only to run out of gainful employment and assets so that you become indigent at age 70.

Fortunately, there's a lot of leeway between those two extremes. When you apply creative lifestyle choices, it releases you from the limitations of conventional planning. This creativity can open the door to living the retirement of your dreams a lot sooner and with a lot more security than you ever imagined possible. I did it myself and so have many of my coaching clients. You can too.

MODEL 3

CASH FLOW PLANNING,
THE SIMPLE WAY

MY SECRET TO A
SECURE RETIREMENT AT AGE 35

"THE ABILITY TO SIMPLIFY MEANS TO ELIMINATE THE UNNEC-
ESSARY SO THAT THE NECESSARY CAN SPEAK."

- HANS HOFFMAN, PAINTER

Now that you understand how to get creative with your assumptions and play with your numbers using nothing more than basic tools, I'll show you my own personal model for retirement planning. It doesn't use any fancy calculators or require arcane assumptions. It is the very same model I used to retire at age 35 with security and confidence.

Truth be told, this book is just an outgrowth of my own journey to determine how much was enough to retire at the ripe old age of 35. I analyzed all the various mathematical models, investigated the required assumptions, and found the whole experience less than satisfying. Hopefully, this compilation of what I learned has helped you shortcut my own lengthy and tedious learning curve.

My early career was developing quantitative risk management models for financial markets, so I had a bit more background than most to bring to this process. I saw firsthand what works and what doesn't when financially modeling an unknowable future, and I've learned that it pays to keep things simple.

Complicated math is usually more symptomatic of covering up ignorance than expressing wisdom. If Einstein could accurately express the mechanics of the universe in a simple equation, then estimating the savings required for retirement should be a little less daunting than conventional wisdom suggests. When I started tinkering with the idea of financial independence in my thirties, I figured there had to be a better way to figure out how much money was enough.

As it turns out, the process is far simpler than any of us have been led to believe. Better yet, the simplest solution also provides the most robust, reliable answer.

Einstein would have been pleased.

The Three Rules

The upshot is that the various assumptions and estimates required by standard models are unnecessary. Instead, you can use a simple three-rule system that bypasses the assumptions mess by *substituting the traditional asset projection model with a cash flow analysis model.*

This crucial distinction is the difference between what I call conventional "treasure chest" planning versus "apple orchard" planning. With the former, you cram gold into a box and hope you don't outlive the pile as you watch the level drop ever lower. With the latter, you plant an orchard (multiple sources of passive income) and live off the apples, but never, ever cut down the trees.

This entire cash flow retirement planning model is so simple it can be summarized in just three rules that don't require any estimates about life expectancy, inflation, or investment return. In fact, you make no assumptions at all because it's entirely based on real-time results.

Here's how it works:

The first rule is that you must build an investment portfolio that generates passive income in excess of personal expenses. Please note that this income doesn't have anything to do with total investment return but only refers to the passive income component. The rule is you can only spend the income thrown off by the assets, but the assets themselves can never be touched. This distinction is important. It's what sets this strategy apart.

When the passive income from your portfolio is more than your living expenses, then you're infinitely wealthy. There's no need for complicated math.

To put this model in practice, you simply acquire assets (real estate, businesses, stocks, mutual funds, annuities, etc.) until the passive income from those assets exceeds your personal expenses. This income can come from a traditional portfolio, or it could come from alternative assets. The asset class and investment strategy is entirely your preference.

All that's important is that your passive income exceeds your expenses. At this point, your life expectancy is irrelevant since you're not at risk of outliving your income. Budgets and lifetime spending forecasts are irrelevant too, because you're only allowed to spend the income your portfolio generates. Your portfolio income defines your budget.

The second rule is that you must manage your assets so that growth (total return minus income) is greater than the inflation rate. Fortunately, this is relatively easy to do over the long term, and it takes care of the inflation monster because the growth component of your portfolio exceeds inflation.

You might achieve this objective with a growing stock portfolio, or it could be less traditional using real estate and business assets. However, what will not work is income coming 100 percent from a laddered bond portfolio[25]. That's because your growth is zero since total return and income roughly equals each other over time. Over the long term, the inflation monster would likely eat your all-bond portfolio for lunch while you live off the fixed income. That's not acceptable.

Alternatively, if your cash comes from appreciating assets like properly valued, dividend-paying stocks and positive cash flow rental real estate, then over time those assets are likely to grow with inflation and your income should likewise grow. As long as the difference between your total return and the income from your assets exceeds the rate of inflation, then you can remove any need to estimate future inflation from your calculations. It becomes a nonissue.

Notice how simple this model is: No longevity estimate, no inflation estimate, no return on investment estimate, and you don't even need to estimate how much money you need to retire. In fact, you don't have to assume anything about the future except what can be reasonably discerned from history. All you have to do is build a portfolio of assets that grows over time with inflation and produces more income than you spend.

The third and final simplifying rule is that your passive income must come from multiple, noncorrelated sources. A reasonable mixture of TIPS, dividend-paying stocks, income-producing real estate, inflation-adjusting fixed annuities, and alternative investment strategies would satisfy that requirement. It's also possible to mix in some passive business income, royalty income, social security income, pension income, and other sources.

What you don't want to do is retire based on one source of income. For example, many airline employees retired solely on their company pensions, only to have them decimated when certain airlines went through bankruptcy and restructuring. They had no fallback position and had to change their lifestyles or go back to work. Similarly, many dotcom millionaires went back to work after the technology stock bust from 2000-2002, as did real estate investors after the 2008-2009 Great Recession.

The message is clear: diversify your assets so if any one source of income gets wiped out, you can still survive comfortably and buy yourself enough time to eventually recover.

You should be no more willing to bet your entire retirement on an insurance company's ability to pay an annuity than you should rely on the government to honor its promises for social security. It's okay to make each one a piece of your retirement equation, but each income source has risks, which must be managed. *Never leave yourself exposed to a single default that can wipe out your financial security.*

A fourth bonus rule also exists, though it isn't mandatory. Think of this bonus rule as an insurance policy against the unknown factors in life ruled by Murphy's Law. To be very conservative, don't retire until your cash flow exceeds what you spend so you have money left over to reinvest for future growth. This provides the last added measure of insurance to cover against unexpected surprises, lost income due to default, catastrophes, excess inflation, etc. Reinvesting excess revenue allows you to compound your way back over time from any adverse circumstances.

There you have it, three simple rules (plus one bonus rule for the very conservative) with no arcane assumptions or calculations. If you can do basic math, you can plan your retirement. And if you stick to your plan, you can retire at any age without worrying about inflation or longevity. You don't have to foresee the future or estimate the impossible. You can absolutely, definitively know when you have enough to retire.

All you have to know is:

- Your current spending

- The income from your assets

- And whether or not those assets tend to grow in value with inflation

It is as simple as simple gets. Best of all, it's robust and totally accurate.

CRITICISM OF THE CASH FLOW RETIREMENT MODEL

Some may disagree with this three-step plan as being too conservative or difficult to achieve. The arguments include the possibility that it might require more assets than other models because you can't spend the principal. This is only true if you remain fully allocated to a conventional paper asset portfolio of stocks, bonds, and mutual funds. Alternative assets like business and real estate could provide the required income without necessarily requiring additional equity.

Another complaint is that you never get to spend your principal, resulting in a larger legacy than you might want. This is valid, but if that concerns you, then just change the rules to include spending from the principal in your later years when life expectancy is 20 years or less. In other words, that's an easily solvable "problem."

Generally, most of the criticism directed at this three-step process comes from financial planners who claim the goal is too lofty for people who got a late start or had an inadequate plan.

I disagree. When an investor focuses on cash flow from assets rather than just accumulating a mountain of retirement accounts, they're naturally directed to consider alternative assets, including real estate and business. These two asset classes just happen to provide the best potential to catch up for investors who got a late start or are behind on savings—the very people that the financial planning profession claim can't apply this model. If this subject interests you then you can learn more about accelerated asset growth strategies in my Expectancy Wealth Planning course at https://financialmentor. com/3.

The relevant point is alternative assets have the potential to deliver higher total returns, resulting in greater equity growth due to taxation and leverage advantages. Many investors find they need less total equity in their portfolio because the yield on their real estate or business exceeds the safe withdrawal rate on their conventional portfolio. Not only that, but their entire portfolio risk profile will likely decrease because the alternative assets improve diversification.

The beauty of this simple, three rule model is it has never been criticized in terms of its validity, robustness, or security—just that it's too lofty. To that I reply, "The math is inviolable." Nobody is served by deception. You can offer easier alternatives that require a lower total savings amount, and you can offer more passive approaches to investment management because they're easier, but that "easiness" comes at the price of greater risk. Unfortunately, you'll never know if that risk will bite you in the rear until it's too late to do anything about it. That's not acceptable.

ADVANTAGES OF THE CASH FLOW RETIREMENT MODEL

Others may prefer the traditional model *because they have greater confidence in making the necessary assumptions than in making the assumptions unnecessary.* It's really a personal choice. At my age, it's easier to build assets than to make assumptions 50 years into the future. Your situation and preferences may be different. Either way, you now have the tools required for all three retirement planning models included in this book.

The main thing to note is how every other model relies on history to be your guide. This cash flow-based model is the only approach that requires no historical analysis *because it is entirely based on numbers fully known in the present*. This is important because the past is not the future.

What I learned from all those years spent researching investment strategy models for the financial markets is that no historically derived investment methodology ever performed in the future like it did in the past. Similarly, no historically derived retirement scenario can be relied on for the future. That's just the reality of financial modeling, and that's why I like the cash flow model—it makes projections about the future irrelevant.

The other reason I like this three-rule model is that the bulk of my assets are nontraditional, so they don't fit well within the confines of traditional retirement planning. However, the flexibility of this super-simple model allows you to combine any and all assets under one analysis. Everything fits, whether it's business, investment property, stocks, bonds, annuities—you name it. All assets fit under one umbrella.

Finally, the last advantage of this three-rule system cannot be overstated: It avoids scarcity consciousness. When retirees spend principal from their portfolio, progressively making their way toward zero assets, a tragic phenomenon occurs: They begin to feel impoverished. It's a natural response to watching your assets dwindle as you spend them down, and it's miserable. After all, you can't exactly call it your "golden years" if you spend your retirement watching every penny.

My three-rule model completely eliminates poverty consciousness because you're only spending income. You feel perpetually wealthy, abundant, and financially secure. The value of this to the quality of your life in retirement cannot be overstated when contrasted with a traditional asset-based, amortization model.

Why It Works

The lesson I've learned through coaching clients on these issues and wrestling with the same in my own life is that most people are focused on a flawed risk model. The real goal is sustainable spending, not portfolio value. That's why this simple cash flow model works so well.

Assets are just a middleman that throw off the income and is at best loosely correlated to what really matters—spendable money to pay the bills. That one sentence packs a lot of punch, so please read it twice. It can change how you plan your retirement. It can change the types of assets you acquire, when you choose to retire, and of course, how much money you need to retire.

That's the other fascinating thing about this three-rule system—it changes your investment strategy because not many assets satisfy all three rules. No longer does it make sense to speculate on stocks going up in value or vacant land deals to build wealth when the focus is directly on acquiring assets to produce cash flow that grows with inflation.

Think about it like this:

- On the fixed-income side of the equation, you'll tend to favor TIPS and inflation-adjusting annuities over traditional bonds, whose fixed payment loses purchasing power over time.

- On the equity side, you'll tend to favor a diversified portfolio of dividend growth stocks over conventional asset allocation based on market capitalization or investment style. Research shows dividends have increased at a rate 2 percent more than inflation, plus the stock portfolio itself grows over time to reflect growth in the world economy.

- Direct ownership of real estate will gain appeal both because it's a tangible asset that increases in value with inflation and because you can't outlive the rental income, which tends to grow with inflation.

In summary, this is one of the simplest, most robust retirement planning strategies in existence. You spend your working career acquiring income-producing assets that grow with inflation until your passive income exceeds your expenses. At that point, you're infinitely wealthy—no assumptions, predictions, or complicated math.

More importantly, it also avoids the scarcity mentality from spending investment principal. It literally overturns every aspect of conventional retirement planning with one critically important shift of perspective from *assets* to *passive income*, and that makes all the difference.

CONCLUSION

"CONTRADICTIONS DO NOT EXIST. WHENEVER YOU THINK YOU ARE FACING A CONTRADICTION, CHECK YOUR PREMISES. YOU WILL FIND THAT ONE OF THEM IS WRONG."

- AYN RAND, WRITER AND PHILOSOPHER

In this book, I've provided you with three different retirement planning models to determine how much money you need to retire:

- **The first model** gave you an extensive depth of knowledge into the problems and challenges with traditional *asset-based retirement planning*. This was essential so you understood the risks associated with this model, plus it set the stage for why the other two models were necessary. In the end, you were given multiple workaround solutions to make the traditional asset-based model usable.

- **The second model** changed the playing field

from financial planning to lifestyle planning by focusing on *assumptions instead of assets*. It included an extensive menu of creative strategies to pick and choose from so you could solve savings shortfalls and retire far earlier with greater financial security than you previously thought possible.

- **The final model** explained my three-rule system for a *cash flow-based retirement* that is simpler and more robust than any other retirement planning model available.

The reason I provided you with all three models is that retirement planning is inherently a bet on an unknowable future so no single solution is definitive. You need a full set of tools to secure your financial future in the face of uncertainty. No single tool is adequate, but all three together provide a definitive solution.

Always remember that the scientific façade of all calculators and the apparent expertise of the financial planning profession masks a host of unknowable assumptions that makes the process as much *art* as *financial science*. As Robert Bengen, one of the pioneers of modern retirement planning said, "*Retirement planning is complex, prone to large errors in estimation, and should embody a large margin for error.*"

Human behavior and the financial markets don't obey "laws" like the physical universe. It's nuanced. Economics is a social science whose knowledge is imprecise, and a practitioner's ability to predict the future is minimal. There are too many factors of varying influence to ever reduce these calculations to scientific precision and avoid compounding errors. It's inherent in the nature of the problem.

But that doesn't mean all is lost—quite the contrary. These three models provide a complete and actionable retirement plan when applied with best practices as taught in this book. While they will never produce a definitive "magic number," this combined strategy is more than good enough to satisfy our objectives.

Some readers express surprise as they reach this conclusion that I spent so much of this book on the first model that is least favored, and so little analysis on the final two models when they offer so much value. This was intentional for three reasons:

1. The first model is the most complex because of all the assumptions involved. It requires a lot of explanation to fully know how to apply it the smart way.

2. Every act of creation is at first an act of destruction. Everyone reading this book begins with knowledge of the traditional model, so it must first be deeply understood to value the importance of the other two models.

3. Finally, the other two models are so simple and robust that they don't require much explanation.

Their simplicity is their elegance, so there's no need to waste your time with unnecessary words just to increase their apparent importance.

Now that you understand all three models, I'd like to conclude by summarizing several robust approaches for using each model that I would be willing to bet my financial security on. Each shows a different dimension to comprehensive retirement planning.

MODEL 1 - TRADITIONAL ASSET-BASED RETIREMENT PLAN

- The conventional approach is best used to **explain your retirement from the asset perspective**. It attempts to show you how many assets you must accumulate.

- I like to use this model in a limited capacity with clients because the model, while problematic, still is useful.

- **It doesn't matter whether you use Monte Carlo or conventional calculators** with this model because all asset-based calculation methods suffer from the same assumption problems. Don't ever assume that changing the calculation methodology will solve the accuracy problem. It won't.

- However, if you **walk your results forward every few years** by replacing assumptions with actual real-time data, that reduces the risk of small errors in assumptions multiplying into fatally large errors in output. Revisiting your retirement plan regularly and updating your numbers is required to make an asset-based model safe.

- Additionally, I would only be willing to **spend principal using an asset-based model for the final 20 years or less** of my expected lifetime. That would mean any retirement longer in duration than 20 years would be cash flow only (Model 3) until that final stage because all asset-based models are too mathematically unstable for safe amortization over periods longer than about 20 years.

- Another way to stabilize the traditional model is to **place "guardrails" around your spending.** That way it never rises above a maximum upper percentage of assets and never falls below a minimum percentage of assets. This helps minimize the risk of overspending or underspending your nest egg as your investment portfolio rises and falls with market fluctuations over the years.

- Similarly, I would encourage you to use a calculator for this model that can **control the growth of spending from inflation** in a way that better reflects what the research shows about real retiree spending habits. My own Ultimate Retirement Calculator (https://financialmentor. com/retirement-calculator) allows you to reduce spending at intervals of your choosing by a selected percentage. This gives you full control over the impact of inflation.

- Finally, a great way to stabilize an asset-based retirement plan is to **manage the longevity risk** using various insurance products as explained in the "buckets of risk" model, adding a longevity annuity, and/or cashing out your free-and-clear home at age 85. Projecting unknowable assumptions over long periods is what makes the traditional model so unstable. Managing the longevity assumption to tightly define the time to 20 years or less greatly stabilizes the model.

MODEL 2 – LIFESTYLE PLAN

- Lifestyle planning isn't really a separate retirement model per se. Instead, it goes straight to the jugular of the traditional model by directly addressing how the assumptions used in the calculation are what matters, not the calculator itself. It still relies on the math framework provided by the other two models, but **it turns the planning logic upside down by focusing on retirement spending rather than retirement income.**

- This is my favorite tool when helping people realize their dreams for financial independence and a fulfilling life because it connects the two. No other approach overtly does this.

- This model delivers the empowering message that there is more than one road to the personal freedom you seek. Focusing on the financial consequences of your lifestyle choices gives you full control over when and how you achieve financial freedom. **You're not bound by conventional assumptions**. You can create your plan to uniquely fit you.

- Not only that, but my experience in working with hundreds of clients is that most people haven't been actively questioning their lifestyle assumptions until they start testing scenarios with this model. Once the **lifetime cost of specific lifestyle choices** is made financially tangible, it often results in dramatic personal change.

- For that reason, I recommend that anyone planning their retirement should actively question every lifestyle assumption so you can model the impact of those changed assumptions, one by one, in your retirement plan. It's my favorite go-to tool for closing savings gaps and helping people find freedom decades earlier than they thought was possible.

MODEL 3 — CASH FLOW RETIREMENT PLAN

- This is my **preferred model for retirement time horizons longer than 20 years**. I created it to manage the 60+ year time horizon I faced when I retired at age 35, more than two decades ago. Because it depends only on information known in real-time, it doesn't require the destabilizing assumptions of traditional retirement planning.

- The **downside to this model** is it requires more assets to achieve the goal if you limit your portfolio to traditional asset allocation, or it involves venturing into nontraditional asset classes like rental real estate and business to improve cash flow and equity growth. These alternative asset classes may not be everyone's preference because they involve greater active participation, but the advantage is they also provide greater diversification when combined with a traditional portfolio, thereby **increasing your security and lowering risk**.

In short, my go-to retirement plan is Model 3 for simplicity, stability, and safety. My favorite retirement planning tool is Model 2 for integrating life plans with financial plans. It's the most effective way to find creative solutions that close savings gaps so you can retire decades earlier than you thought was possible. And I like Model 1 for highlighting the asset side of the equation and for modeling scenarios with the ideas from Model 2.

Each model progressively adds important knowledge and a critical dimension to your retirement planning process. Your complete retirement plan will combine elements from all three models to deliver a secure and fulfilling post-work life in the shortest possible time.

You're now armed with the knowledge and tools necessary to make an educated and well-reasoned plan that fits your personal situation and secures your financial future. My sincere hope is you will put all of this knowledge to work in building an abundant and financially prosperous retirement so you can live a happy and fulfilled life.

Nobody ever saved for retirement because they wanted more money. Instead, what you want is what you believe that money can buy you. The real goal is freedom, security, and fulfillment by living life on your own terms.

I hope this book helps you live your dreams.

BONUS CONTENT

This book is not just what you hold in your hands. There's so much more that I wanted to include but couldn't due to formatting limitations and editorial requirements. Fortunately, your purchase gives you full access to these additional free resources at https://financialmentor.com/free-stuff/retirement-book.

- **Workbook:** A conveniently-formatted printable PDF workbook containing fill-in-the-blank forms for all the exercises and action steps included in this book. The workbook will help you:

    - Complete the various calculations in the book

    - Estimate and track your assumptions

    - Calculate your confidence interval

    - Record essential data from various parts of the book for use with online retirement calculators

- **Bonus Chapters:** A PDF e-book containing the following bonus chapters:

  - *How Anyone Can Retire in 10 Years… or Less!*

  - *The One-Minute Retirement Plan*

  - *5 Essential Questions for Preretirement Planning*

  - *Twelve Tips to Systematically Build Your Wealth Faster For Early Retirement*

  - *Retirement Planning Checklist*

- **Wealth Plan:** A sample Wealth Plan taken from my Expectancy Wealth Planning course, complete with instructional tips to create one for yourself.

You can claim your bonuses now at https://financial mentor.com/free-stuff/retirement-book.

AFTERWORD

If you felt this book delivered on its promise, please share a quick review where you purchased it.

Your review truly matters and doesn't have to be complicated. Just a quick two to three sentences sharing book highlights or what you learned to help others know if the book is helpful or not. It's a great way to give back and make a difference.

GLOSSARY

No financial education book can perfectly address every reader's needs. After all, each of us brings a different level of financial experience to the written page. What is complicated to one person may seem oversimplified to the next.

To maintain brevity and respect all readers' needs, I assumed base-level financial knowledge and offer definitions here for less familiar terms referenced in the text.

1. **Market Valuation:** The price at which investors buy or sell common stock and bonds in the market relative to a fundamental indicator. Typical measures include price/earnings ratios, Q ratio, price/dividend ratio, price/sales ratio, and more. A high market valuation indicates a high price relative to underlying business fundamentals, and a low valuation indicates a low price relative to underlying business fundamentals.

2. **Monte Carlo**: An analytical method used to estimate the probability of certain outcomes occurring by running a large number of simulations using random variables.

The resulting output is expressed as a confidence interval intended to quantify the percentage of times that your money would last beyond your life expectancy.

3. **Confidence Interval:** Attempts to define a range within which the desired answer is estimated and its precision. Used when single-point estimates are not sufficiently reliable for decision making, it measures the probability that a value will fall between an upper or lower boundary. For example, a 95 percent confidence interval means that 95 times out of 100, the result should be within the upper and lower boundary of the range, and 5 times out of 100, the result should fall outside the range.

4. **Backcast:** An attempt to estimate a potential future outcome by testing backward on historical data.

5. **Average Return:** The rate of return computed by adding all the individual returns together and then dividing by the quantity of individual returns in the set.

6. **S&P 500 Index:** A market value-weighted index of 500 stocks chosen by analysts at Standard and Poor's corporation.

7. **Safe Withdrawal Rate:** The highest withdrawal rate, expressed as a percentage of the account balance on the first day of retirement and adjusted for inflation annually. It allows for a lifetime of withdrawals without running out of money before you run out of life.

Glossary

8. **Investment Holding Period:** The amount of time between purchase and sale that an investor owned a security.

9. **P/E:** The ratio of market price for a company's stock divided by its earnings per share. It represents how much investors are paying for that company's earnings stream.

10. **CAPE:** Popularized by Robert Shiller from Yale University, CAPE is the ratio of stock prices to the moving average of the previous 10 years' earnings, deflated by the consumer price index. It's a popular measure of market valuation because the 10-year average typically measures over a full market cycle, thereby increasing reliability when contrasted with shorter-term measures.

11. **Quintile:** The portion of a distribution containing 1/5 (or 20 percent) of the total.

12. **Compound Return:** The rate of return expressed as an annual percentage, representing the cumulative change in value from the daily gains and losses, and earning a return on themselves.

13. **Dollar-Cost Averaging:** A method of investing a fixed amount of money on a regular schedule, regardless of price. It causes more shares to be purchased when prices are low and fewer shares to be purchased when prices are high.

14. **Quartile:** The portion of a distribution containing 1/4 (or 25 percent) of the total.

15. **Capitalization Rate:** Often called just the Cap Rate, it's a valuation measure used to compare different real estate investments. It's calculated by dividing the net operating income, or NOI, by the property value. It's used to indicate the expected rate of return on a real estate investment property.

16. **Gross Rent Multiplier:** GRM is the ratio of the purchase price of a property to its gross income—before accounting for expenses like taxes, insurance, and maintenance. It indicates the number of years the property would take to pay for itself and can be used to compare properties for relative investment merit.

17. **Large-Cap Equities:** Stocks with a market capitalization greater than $10 billion.

18. **Dividend Growth Stocks:** Equities of companies with expanding earnings and sales that increase their dividend payout to investors regularly.

19. **Fixed Annuity:** An insurance contract providing a fixed payment stream for life in exchange for a single lump-sum purchase. An optional feature is to increase the payments over time based on the rate of inflation to protect purchasing power for the investor.

20. **Hedge Fund:** A private investment pool usually arranged as a partnership and subject to accredited investor rules to qualify for investment. Hedge funds will typically employ complex investment strategies, leverage, and/or derivative securities to try and earn noncorrelated

and above-market investment returns to justify their above-market fees and liquidity limitations.

21. **TIPS:** Treasury Inflation-Protected Securities are bonds issued by the US Treasury in 5, 10, and 20-year maturities. They provide a fixed interest rate, but the principal value indexes to inflation to protect purchasing power.

22. **Equity Allocation:** A strategy of apportioning an investment portfolio between various asset classes (e.g., stocks, bonds, cash) that attempts to match risk and reward to the investor's goals and risk tolerance.

23. **Annuitize:** To convert a sum of money into a series of payments.

24. **Longevity Insurance Annuity:** An immediate annuity that defers payments until a future date. For example, an annuitant could purchase longevity insurance at age 65 that pays $5,000 per month beginning at age 85.

25. **Laddered Bond Portfolio:** A portfolio of fixed income securities with evenly spaced maturity dates. The objective is to reduce interest rate risk.

ABOUT THE AUTHOR

Todd R. Tresidder's financial writing has been featured in the Wall Street Journal, Smart Money Magazine, Investor's Business Daily, Forbes, Yahoo Finance, Inc., USA Today, and more. He is a former hedge fund manager who "retired" at age 35 to become a financial consumer advocate and money coach. In his spare time he's an outdoor recreational enthusiast with varied interests from backpacking and adventure travel to endurance running and cycling. He writes nine months of the year from his home in Reno, Nevada while his kids are in school, and he plays the rest of the year. You can learn more about Todd at financialmentor.com.

ADDITIONAL BOOKS BY TODD TRESIDDER

The Leverage Equation
The Missing Tool That Unblocks your Success,
So You Can Make More By Working Less

The 4% Rule and Safe Withdrawal Rates In Retirement

Variable Annuity Pros & Cons
Surprising Truths Your Advisor Won't Tell You

Investment Fraud
How Financial "Experts" Rip You Off
and What To Do About It

Don't Hire a Financial Coach!
(Until You Read This Book)

ADDITIONAL COURSES BY TODD TRESIDDER

Expectancy Wealth Planning
Advanced Wealth Growth Strategies
to Accelerate Your Freedom

Retirement Calculator Secrets
The Coolest Calculator Tricks Nobody Ever Taught You
for Getting Your Number Right
and Securing Your Financial Future

CPSIA information can be obtained
at www.ICGtesting.com
Printed in the USA
BVHW070809190820
586727BV00004B/4